MONTEREY JAZZ FESTIVAL

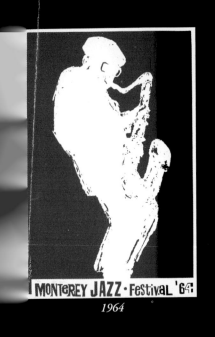
1964

1964

1967

1984

1985

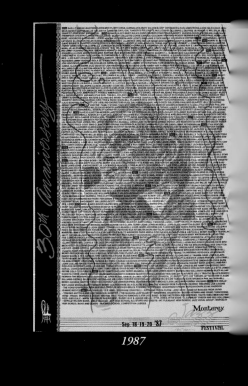
1987

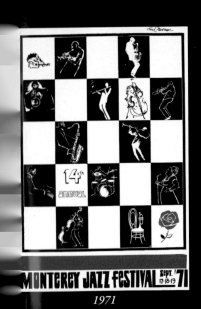
1971

1978

MONTEREY JAZZ FESTIVAL
SEPTEMBER 19-20-21
1980

1980

1993

1994

1996

1979

THE MONTEREY JAZZ FESTIVAL SILVER ANNIVERSARY
SEPTEMBER 17, 18 & 19, 1982

The 1995 Monterey Jazz Festival
1995

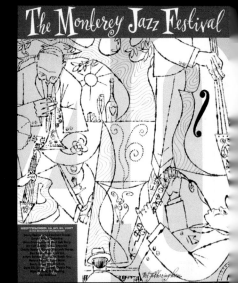
Presented by MCI

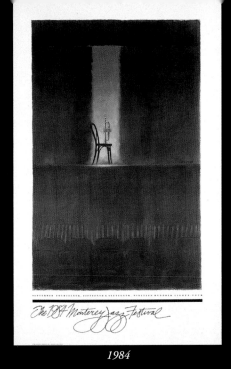

MONTEREY JAZZ FESTIVAL

FORTY LEGENDARY YEARS

WILLIAM MINOR

Photography Editor BILL WISHNER

Foreword by CLINT EASTWOOD

Design by JEFF DARNALL/SDA

ANGEL CITY PRESS

Welcome to this celebration of forty years of the Monterey Jazz Festival. MCI Communications Corporation is indeed proud and honored by our association with the Festival, now going on thirteen years.

As individuals, and as a corporation, we at MCI are drawn to the Monterey Jazz Festival for a number of reasons. For one thing, its commitment to education is a commitment we share. The Festival's Jazz Education Fund, a continuing program of jazz education throughout Monterey County, brings this most expressive medium to young people. And from coast to coast, in schools and in libraries, MCI brings to young people the most powerful new medium, the Internet.

But above all, as a global communications company, MCI is all about fostering communication, helping people make connections. And nothing connects like jazz. Jazz is the quintessentially American form of music that has caught on across the globe. Jazz riffs and rhythms connect people from Rio to Riyadh. Its syncopation serves to unite people across class, ethnic and geographic boundaries. Its improvisations display, like nothing else, the sheer playfulness of human creativity.

And that's the ultimate point about jazz: it connects us with levels of ourselves that otherwise remain hidden. And that's the reason MCI is so proud and honored to be a sponsor of the Monterey Jazz Festival.

Bert C. Roberts, Jr.
Chairman
MCI Communications Corporation

ANGEL CITY PRESS, INC.
Published by Angel City Press
2118 Wilshire Boulevard, Suite 880
Santa Monica, California 90403
(310) 395-9982
http://www.angelcitypress.com

First published in 1997 by Angel City Press
1 3 5 7 9 10 8 6 4 2
FIRST EDITION
ISBN 1-883318-40-8

MONTEREY JAZZ FESTIVAL
FORTY LEGENDARY YEARS
Copyright © 1997 Monterey Jazz Festival
Text by William Minor
Photography Editor Bill Wishner
Designed by Jeff Darnall

Library of Congress Cataloging-in-Publication Data

Minor, William, 1936-
    Monterey Jazz Festival : Forty Legendary Years / by William Minor and Bill Wishner.   -- 1st ed.
        p.   cm.
    Includes bibliographical references and index.
    ISBN 1-883318-40-8
    1. Monterey Jazz Festival. 2. Jazz--California--Monterey--History and criticism. I. Title.
    ML38.M657M64 1997
    781.65'079'79476--dc21   97-4908
                                                                                          CIP
                                                                                          MN

....

To Jimmy Lyons

1916 – 1994

Founder

of the

Monterey Jazz Festival

ACKNOWLEDGMENTS

Within a seven month period – September 1996 through March 1997 – I conducted fifty-one interviews with musicians, members of the Board of Directors (past and present), Festival personnel, long-term fans, and media representatives. I also, prior to that time, working on a project on jazz in Japan, interviewed six musicians who had performed at the Monterey Jazz Festival. Nearly all of the interviews were taped, and are now the property of the Festival archives. I would like to thank the following musicians for their participation in this project:

Dave Brubeck, John Lewis, Percy Heath, Max Roach, Ray Brown, Jon Hendricks, Mundell Lowe, David Friesen, Toshiko Akiyoshi, Clark Terry, Billy Childs, Maria Schneider, James Williams, Don Schamber, Bill Berry, Bruce Forman, Bunky Green, Kitty Margolis, Ann Dyer, Eiji Kitamura, Kotaro Tsukahara, Yoshiaki (Miya) Miyanoue, Sumi Tonooka and Benny Green.

I would also like to thank the following Board members, Festival personnel and "family," long-term fans, photographers and jazz journalists:

Tim Jackson, Joe Green, Jim Costello, Grover Sales, Paul Vieregge, Ernie Beyl, Laurel Lyons, George "Bob" Faul, Sam Karas, Biff Smith, Darlene Chan, David Murray, Mary Piazza, Stella LePine, Dee Dee Rainbow, Bill Lindsay, Naomi Meyer, Hans Lehmann, John McCleary, Harry Crawford, Nick Williams, Bill Welch, Peter Breinig, Herb Wong, Phil Elwood, David Gitin, Ray March, Rick Carroll, Scott Yanow, Ray Avery, Will Wallace, John Detro and Dan Ouellette.

I also made several trips to the Stanford University Libraries Archive of Recorded Sound, and would like to thank Barbara Sawka for making my listening sessions there possible. I would especially like to thank Aurora Perez for her patience, agility with Q-tips (cleaning heads for the best possible sound) and astute conversational asides.

The Monterey Jazz Festival office print media archives offered valuable information, and I am grateful to the following writers and the publications in which their work originally appeared: Dick Hadlock (*The Jazz Review*), Ralph J. Gleason (*San Francisco Chronicle, Saturday Review*), Gene Lees (*Down Beat*), Grover Sales (*San Francisco Town and Country; Jazz: A Quarterly of American Music*, edited by Ralph J. Gleason), John Tynan (*Down Beat*), R.J. Tinkham (*Audio Magazine*), Russ Wilson (*Oakland Tribune*), Stanley Dance (*Metronome*), Nat Hentoff (*Playboy*), Don DeMicheal (*Down Beat*), Whitney Balliett (*New Yorker*), Dan Morgenstern (*Down Beat*), Willis Conover (*Saturday Review*), Leonard Feather (*Down Beat, Los Angeles Times, JazzTimes*), Ray Townley and Herb Wong (*Down Beat*), Harvey Siders *(Down Beat)*, Langdon Winner (*Rolling Stone*), Len Lyons (*Down Beat*), Philip Elwood (*San Francisco Examiner*), Allen Scott and Miles Jordan (*Radio Free Jazz*), Grover Lewis *(New West)*, Zan Stewart (*Down Beat*), Eliot Tiegel (*Billboard*), Conrad Silvert (*San Francisco Chronicle*), Rick Carroll (*Monterey Peninsula Herald*), Steve Eddy (*Orange County Register*), Joel Selvin (*San Francisco Chronicle*), A. James Liska (*Van Nuys Valley News*), Scott Yanow (*L.A. Jazz Scene*), Terre Lyons (*Carmel Pine Cone*), Thomas Conrad (*Down* Beat), Charles Levin (*Santa Cruz County Sentinel*), Al Goodman (*Monterey Peninsula* Herald), John Detro (*Carmel Pine Cone*), Jill Duman (*Coast Weekly*), Mac McDonald (*Monterey Peninsula Herald*).

The following writers have contributed to the Festival program, and I would like to thank them for information they provided: Ralph J. Gleason, Grover Sales, Ernie Beyl, Vicky Cunningham, Herb Wong, Len Lyons, Leonard Feather, Phil Elwood, Paul S. Fingerote, Paul Vieregge, Ray A. March, Bob Michael, Samantha Roby, Dan Kassis, John Detro, Rick Carroll, Jesse Hamlin, Charles Levin, Jeff Kaliss, Mike Burck, Jill Duman, Tom Owens, Dan Ouellette and Ira Kamin.

Dizzy, Duke, The Count and Me, by Jimmy Lyons with Ira Kamin (A California Living Book; The San Francisco Examiner Division of The Hearst Corporation, 1978) was a valuable source of information and anecdotes. John Detro's poem "The Radio Man" first appeared in *When All the Wild Summer* (Holmgangers Press, 1983). Special thanks to my colleague Scott Yanow, the value of whose massive contribution to the *All Music Guide to Jazz* (Miller Freeman Books, 1996) is exceeded only by his good company. Our Festival paths first crossed in 1987, and he has since provided much wit and wisdom.

Thanks to my partner in this project, Bill Wishner, who collected the many handsome photographs, and to Jeff Darnall, of Samuels Darnall & Associates for the book's fine design. I would also like to thank the good shepherds, the guiding spirits at Angel City Press: Scott McAuley, Jean Penn, Andrea Dovichi, Jane Centofante and especially my editor, Paddy Calistro, with whom it was a pleasure to work on this project. And always: to my mother, Dorothy, to Betty, Tim, Janice, Emily, Blake, Steve and Yoko – without whom even jazz would be less bright in this life. **–William Minor**

TABLE OF CONTENTS

In 1958, thousands crowded the Main Arena to watch the Festival's first performances on an austere, makeshift stage.

FOREWORD

By Clint Eastwood

I've been a jazz fan as far back as I can remember. When I was twelve years old, living in Oakland, California, I discovered a radio program called Dixieland Jubilee, and that was the beginning. I started going to jazz concerts and clubs in the Bay Area even though I was too young to drink; it was the music that attracted me.

I came to Monterey for the first time in 1951, when I was in the military. It was a quiet place then, but I saw a few players at the old Blue Ox and the Casa Munras. On weekends I would go into San Francisco to hear Mulligan, Brubeck and all the guys playing there. It was a great time for jazz and the Bay Area influence was spreading.

When I got out of the service I kept coming back to the Monterey Peninsula, even when I was in college in southern California. And when I heard that there was going to be a jazz festival in Monterey I came up for it.

The first Monterey Jazz Festival was more like a fair than a series of planned concerts. It was a much smaller event than now, centered in the main arena of the fairgrounds. Typical of events of that era, the sound system didn't always work, and someone would always be coming out on stage tapping on the microphones or blowing into them. There was feedback, a lot of fog and old-time planes were flying in; but everyone had a good time. It was the beginning of something that kept on growing.

I came back to the Jazz Festival over the years and always enjoyed myself. Then, in 1970, I was directing my first film, *Play Misty for Me*, and I needed an event as a transition in the film. Since the Festival was happening in Monterey at the time, I thought we might be able to film in the middle of the fairgrounds, where lots of things were going on, to create the backdrop for a suspense turning point.

I went to talk to Jimmy Lyons who was the head of the Festival, about filming there. At that point I had known of Jimmy since the 1940s. He had a jazz radio program in San Francisco and he played some good stuff. That was the time of the introduction of Shearing and Brubeck and all that West Coast sound, and Jimmy was right there with it.

Jimmy was great about my request. He suggested the blues afternoon because of the colorful clothes that people wore and the fact that the audience usually got up and danced to that music. So that's what we filmed and, later that day, we shot Cannonball Adderley, one of my favorite alto sax players. In the end, jazz played a big part in that movie and in my subsequent films.

When I moved up to the Peninsula in the 1960s, the Monterey Jazz Festival was a big thing to look forward to each year. We liked the Bach Festival in Carmel and the Jazz Festival at the Monterey Fairgrounds; those were the key events during the year. My son Kyle was introduced to the Festival at an early age, and last year he made his second appearance there as a performer, which was a real thrill for both of us.

Clint Eastwood and Donna Mills take a break from filming Play Misty For Me *(1971), directed by and starring Eastwood. The 1970 Johnny Otis blues show featuring Jimmy Rushing, Big Joe Turner and Little Esther Phillips provided Saturday afternoon backdrop.*

Today the Jazz Festival has grown to fill the whole fairgrounds; it's a world-famous gathering. Now you can wander from venue to venue and grab a bite to eat in between, which is nice, but sometimes it's frustrating to realize that there are so many great acts going on simultaneously that you can't possibly hear them all. Still, you do the best you can and hope that you'll catch the performances you missed when the players come back another year.

The Monterey Jazz Festival has had so much history that over time its bugs have been worked out and now it's a world-class festival. In the early days when jazz was less serious, there used to be many jam sessions late into the nights. In the Seventies and Eighties everyone got serious – maybe too serious, because jazz is bluesy and forlorn, but also happy and upbeat. Today I'm glad to see that there seems to be a shift back to that feeling of celebration in jazz.

As you turn the pages of this book, I hope you'll feel the celebration in jazz at Monterey, those forty years of the shaping of Jimmy Lyons' dream into what is now a great festival. Many who are no longer with us have contributed to the success of the Monterey Jazz Festival and to the memories that so many of us carry. And in those ranks are countless legends of the jazz world whose contributions to music and to Monterey are unforgettable. The many photographs and recollections included here celebrate those first forty years and the promise of more to come.

INTRODUCTION

Strolling the grounds – the sounds of an inspired set by Charlie Haden's Liberation Music Orchestra or Sonny Rollins or Chick Corea still vivid in your mind – you might feel the Monterey Jazz Festival, with its mild Central California Coast setting and timeless music, came into being all of a piece, without struggle. Nothing – nobody – turns forty without a history of pain and pleasure, frustration and victory. But right now it all seems so perfect, spontaneous and whole, like those offspring of the mythological gods who emerged fully formed at birth.

As you exit the arena that houses the Jimmy Lyons Stage, you are greeted by two long rows of vendors' booths, situated on different ground levels to your left. Their wares sparkle now in the bright light that pierces through the surrounding live-oak trees. At an African arts concession, you discover burnished olive wood and rich ebony masks and figurines; then brilliant red, orange and purple sarongs and silk scarves at another booth. The Monterey Jazz Festival's international repute and flavor are further reflected, not only in crafts from Tibet, Senegal, Kenya, Bali, Israel, Guatemala, Mexico, and Ireland (jewelry, soapstones, batiks, incense, lotions, glass sculpture, musical instruments), but also by the forty Australians and one hundred fans who've come all the way from Japan to join the crowd that strolls beside you. Don't be surprised to overhear a local resident tell friends he's just made, "When I was traveling in Russia and told people that I was from Monterey, they always replied, "Oh, *that's* where they have the famous jazz festival!"

Hungry and thirsty, you head back up

the midway, past cranberry-colored zodiac rugs; magenta, black and orange "jazz cats" blankets, a variety of refrigerator magnets on display at Aunt Gert's Collectibles; posters depicting dramatic black-and-white photographs of every jazz great from John Coltrane to Louis Armstrong, Art Blakey to Billie Holiday – all of whom graced the Festival Main Stage at one time or another in the event's forty-year history. You pass a large Tower Records pavilion, where fans have flocked for the latest CD (and possibly an autograph) of an exciting performer they've just discovered at one of the five musical venues the Festival grounds provide. You work your way among a colorful crowd decked out in anything from zebra pattern off-the-shoulder robes and wide-brimmed hats to ankle-length leather coats, or even just halters and jeans. You spot some of the musicians you heard earlier – look, there's Clark Terry! There's Hank Jones! Or silver-haired Eiji Kitamura with his familiar pipe. You may even stumble upon some celebrity fans, or at least hear long-term Festival fans nearby discuss the time they saw Kim Novak and Wilt Chamberlain together, or ran into Steve McQueen, who had just driven up from L.A. on his motorcycle.

Suddenly you smell, and spot, the food: Smokin' Jim's dark red rib slabs sitting invitingly atop a sprawling rack. A whole pig, its sleek mauve sides roasting on a spit, turns in time to a sensuous ballad sung by Rebecca Parris or Mary Stallings, off to your right, in the open shell of the Garden Stage tucked behind the booths. Strolling toward the fairgrounds' north end, you pass a range of cuisine that, again, reflects the Festival's international character:

ABOVE: A midway poet espouses his poetical/political cause in the Festival's early days. Before five fairground venues provided full-time music, the midway offered everything from juggling acts to Jazzercise demonstrations to "street performers." OPPOSITE: Dizzy Gillespie, shown here warming up backstage, became a Festival habitue, a regular who claimed that his face was as much a part of the Monterey Jazz Festival as "that chair that they have," the event's logo. The beaded North African cap, the bent trumpet (the result of an early Fifties incident when a dancer accidentally tripped over his horn), the well-traveled mute and balloon cheeks were all trademarks that made up the "face" of this superb musician and master showman.

Thai chicken on a stick, Cajun shrimp, Aidell's Sausage, the Cypress Bake Shop, Bill Welch's Louisiana Catfish, calamari straight from Monterey's own wharf. Knights of Columbus and the Arab Club share adjoining food booths. All these culinary delights mingle with concession stands selling used blues records, a massage tent where fans take time off to get the night chill worked out of their shoulders; the Yamaha pavilion, where – on a grand piano – a couple of journalists abandon their note taking long enough to plunk out an amateur version of "Honeysuckle Rose." Further on, the MCI press tent stands, where earlier in the day a serious, yet relaxed and convivial, press conference was held with Max Roach, Jon Hendricks or Cedar Walton, the latter discussing the commissioned piece he would perform that night, "Autumn Sketches."

Having eaten your fill, it's time to enjoy some of the liquid refreshment available at one of the makeshift bars that dot the grounds. Dined and wined, you head up the midway, the overhead light more subdued here, the oak trees more abundant, past young hopefuls – members of the California High School All-Star Big Band – picnicking with their families atop a bass drum case. You pass members of a Japanese big band – all the way from Toyama or Gunma or Osaka – having their group picture taken after completing a hot set in your destination: the Night Club. There, within its dark intimate space, Jessica Williams offers her brilliant reflective piano stylings, or trumpeter Roy Hargrove and pianist Billy Childs pair up for a spontaneous but inspired set of jazz standards. Directly across from the Night Club, up a small hill, you find Dizzy's Den, where you are drawn by the blazing sounds of Charlie Hunter's Trio, or veteran alto saxophonist Lou Donaldson, or – if you're lucky – you're on hand to partake of that memorable night when tenor saxophonist Eddie Harris and guitarist Bruce Forman joined the sweet as velour, tart as lemon sounds of Dr. Lonnie Smith and Johnny "Hammond" Smith in an organ jam. Emerging from Dizzy's Den, you notice free three-minute phone calls are being placed to Paris or Michigan via Festival sponsor MCI, and you decide to make one yourself, to your mother or a faraway best friend.

Strolling back down the midway, delighted with everything, taking your time, you realize that the Monterey Jazz Festival is *the* American jazz event, legendary but alive, the oldest continuous jazz festival in the world. Walking the grounds, you are reminded of this when you catch a glimpse of a musical artist such as the renowned Ray Brown, who first performed here in 1959 as bassist with the Oscar Peterson Trio. Standing outside the Festival's office, Brown is swapping stories with musicians he hasn't seen for a year. He's telling them about the time he was standing, just like this, thirty-one years ago, chatting with the Festival's co-founder and then general manager, Jimmy Lyons. Brown was Lyons' musical director in 1966, a wild time in the Festival's history when, as the bassist tells it now, fans were "carrying on so bad the neighbors complained to the police." While Brown was chatting with Lyons, "this guy walks up with all these medals on his chest. Monterey's chief of police. He looks around and he says, 'Who's running this thing?' And Jimmy points to *me*. He points to me and the chief says, 'What's your name?' I said, 'Brown.' And he said, 'All right, Mr. Brown. I want this show shut down by midnight. And if it isn't, I'm going to put you in jail.' And he walked away." The bassist goes on to tell how Jimmy Lyons allowed the joke to go so far that, after Brown had convinced Count Basie and the sometimes irascible singer Carmen McRae ("You know how evil she could be," Brown reminds his fellow musicians) to limit their sets, he was accused of "Crow Jim" tactics by Gerry Mulligan, who thought his show was being cut just because he was white. "Man," Brown says, "Gerry had a complete conniption, and Jimmy just stood back and smiled." The musicians laugh, fondly recalling the past and all those named.

Such tales can be heard throughout the fairgrounds. After forty years, the Festival is chock full of folklore. Seated at picnic tables scattered not far from the Festival office, fans tell stories people love to tell and love to hear, over and over and over again, converting actual historical events into permanent legends. Like motif types in genuine folklore, these tales have been given titles or names. There's "The Night the Lights Went Out" for example. On opening night in 1979, a power failure plunged the arena in darkness. Dizzy Gillespie was left standing alone on stage, "illuminated only by distant, flickering emergency lights, with no amplification whatsoever," a jazz writer leans across a table to remind his friends. Gillespie was playing "'Round Midnight" as the crowd lit lighters and matches and tenor saxophonist Stan Getz took it upon himself to saunter out, his customary breath-resonant tone an eerily

BELOW: Legendary performers such as, left to right, Rex Stewart, Benny Carter, and Ben Webster have left the indelible stamp of their music on the Festival's history. The full roster of performers reads like a Who's Who of jazz. OPPOSITE: In its early years, the Monterey Jazz Festival pledged to avoid the hackneyed and the trite by coupling musicians who ordinarily didn't have a chance to play together. The 1959 Festival found the searing trumpet of Roy Eldridge paired with Woody Herman's clarinet, both backed by the piano of Earl "Fatha" Hines.

BELOW: Musicians, fans from all over the world, and media personnel mingle on the Festival grounds. Here, pianist Denny Zeitlin is interviewed by Voice of America deejay Willis Conover. OPPOSITE: The Festival midway offers fans a wide range of culinary delights. One of the all-time favorites is barbecued ribs.

comforting whisper in the dark night. Inside the Hunt Club – a VIP bar area reserved for musicians, their families and friends, journalists, photographers, and box-seat ticket holders – someone inspired by Scotch and soda is retelling one of many "Airplane" incidents, this one about the time, at the first Festival, a plane bound for Monterey Airport, and coming in low, passed directly over the Main Stage. Without dropping a beat, pianist Dave Brubeck suddenly played a few bars of "Wild Blue Yonder," alto saxophonist Paul Desmond joining in. Then there are the numerous "Monk" tales: stories centered on the brilliant but eccentric pianist Thelonious Monk. One is about the night the sound system mysteriously shut down until stagehands discovered the source of the problem. Monk had hung his heavy overcoat on the mike.

As you emerge from the Hunt Club, you see a couple of die-hard scalpers hawking tickets for the night's remaining shows. That afternoon, when you arrived at the fairgrounds, a host of scalpers stood by the gate, pitching their wares. You recall the afternoon heat during the blues show, Solomon Burke in his orange-gold-ocher suit that glistened like tinfoil requesting a golf cart at the close of his set so he could ride amongst what he called "his people," the fans he'd set emotionally aflame with

the blues. You smile, thinking of the contrast between the heat of the day and the blues and the cool music of this night.

Some of the people around you seem to know exactly why they are here. They have known for years, maybe all the way back to that first night in 1958. Indeed, they seem to know every musician who's ever performed by name, and the date of every appearance. Other fans look as if they're attending for the first time. For them, perhaps, the Festival is an "in" thing they read about in the morning paper. They drift somewhat aimlessly from venue to venue, but that's okay. That's what you're doing too, for the moment, just taking in all the sounds and sights. Amused, you recall how earlier that evening, attending the performance of the exciting young drummer Leon Parker (who can get more music out of a snare drum and a single cymbal than many percussionists can out of a full drum kit), a group of revelers – obviously having enjoyed the Festival's party side for several hours – took seats in your row. The large man who'd squeezed in next to you leaned over and said, "Who's this?" "Leon Parker," you replied, attempting to tune in on the drummer's host of subtle effects. "Blues?" "No," you reply, "he's a bit . . . well, *out*." "Out?" "Different," you respond. "Different?" "He's not

mainstream," you say, "but . . . *avant-garde.*" "Oh," the man says, then turning to his friends, says, "Avant-garde." They nod knowingly, but ten minutes later, they leave. You smile, knowing that – sometime in the night – they'll find some "blues" to fit their taste, and their party will not stop.

As you stroll back down the midway, you sense – above perhaps but not beyond it all – the presence of those legends who survive time like revered ancestors, their sounds still lingering in the air: Duke, Miles, Sarah, Dizzy. Grateful for a prodigious musical present, you're also cognizant of all the great musicians who graced a Festival stage: Louis Armstrong, Cal Tjader, Harry James, Billie Holiday, Earl "Fatha" Hines, Ben Webster, Coleman Hawkins, Woody Herman, Count Basie, Eric Dolphy, John Coltrane, Wes Montgomery, Cannonball Adderley. The list goes on and on, and you smile, again, pleasantly inundated with the event's history, its evolution – continuity and continuance.

You open your program and see the riches offered throughout the weekend, the river of moments you're moving in. Ornette Coleman & Prime Time and Max Roach and M'Boom. Or perhaps it's Gene Harris, John Scofield, Bobby McFerrin, Toots Thielemans. Or Jon Faddis playing solo trumpet in his mentor Dizzy's stead on Lalo Schifrin's "Gillespiana," Jon Hendricks' re-creation of "Evolution of the Blues" with Dianne Reeves and the great Joe Williams, the Herbie Hancock Quartet with Joshua Redman sitting in.

The immortals among us! So much imperishable music! You check your program once again and discover that the excellent Cecilia Coleman Quintet is now playing on the Garden Stage, fine pianist Laszlo Gardony – with his Hungarian-based rhythms – is at the Night Club, and the miraculous Stephane Grappelli from France is appearing on the Jimmy Lyons Stage. So much to choose from. What'll it be? You want to see and hear them all – and you just might do that. The very best jazz musicians have been, are, and will be at the legendary Monterey Jazz Festival, so you're bound to come up with much to love, as people have for forty years – always coming back for more.

THE LEGEND
BEGINS

On a chilly Friday, October 3, 1958, Louis
Armstrong and his All-Stars strolled on stage at
the Monterey Jazz Festival to play the last set
of opening night. The crowd watched eagerly,
inquisitively, as the great fifty-seven-year-old
classic jazz trumpeter was introduced by a
zany, unpredictable forty-one-year-old emcee
appropriately named "Dizzy." John Birks
"Dizzy" Gillespie got down on his knees, then
rose and kissed Armstrong's hand. Many people in the audience thought he was clowning,
but he wasn't. Gillespie worshiped the man he
called "Pops." These two icons, leaders of their
respective schools – classic jazz, or Dixieland,
and bebop – merged in that magic moment,
the kind people came to expect during the next
forty years of the Monterey Jazz Festival.

That first night ended with Armstrong,
the older master, but it began with Gillespie,
the new. None of the jazz super stars invited to
the Festival wanted to be first on the bill. Gerry
Mulligan, Dave Brubeck, Cal Tjader, Billie
Holiday, Harry James, Max Roach, the Modern
Jazz Quartet, and Armstrong all declined to
serve as a warmup act. But not Gillespie, who
said, "Hell, I'll open it." After muffing the first
notes of "The Star-Spangled Banner," he recov-
ered sufficiently to find his proper register, let
those bombs burst in air, skipped his way
through "the ramparts we watch," and ended
on a stirring quaver.

As emcee, Gillespie took to his chores
with great relish. First he thanked the crowd for
coming. "It means money in our pockets," he
admitted. He then went on to compare the
Monterey event to its rival, the Newport Jazz
Festival, which had started four years before.

*ABOVE: Gregory Millar conducts the Modern Jazz Quartet with the Monterey Jazz Festival
Symphony. The stage at the first Festival was set. An outdoor sound system capable of pro-
jecting hi-fi music to 7300 patrons was installed. Audio Magazine devoted four pages to
what they described as "probably the largest outdoor stereophonic sound reinforcement and
recording system used to date." OPPOSITE: The great trumpeter Louis Armstrong appeared
with his All-Stars and vocalist Velma Middleton on opening night at the first Festival.
Armstrong would return in 1962 and 1965. He always signed his letters to Jimmy Lyons,
"Red beans and ricely yours."*

ABOVE: On the first Festival's closing night, popular comedian Mort Sahl served as emcee. Looking out over the large arena crowd, he drew solid laughter when he stated, "My agent keeps telling me I can't play big rooms."
RIGHT: A surprised Louis Armstrong responds to the homage being paid to him when introduced by the opening night emcee, Dizzy Gillespie.
OPPOSITE: Dressed in a fur to fend off the October chill, singer Billie Holiday made her first, and only, appearance at the Festival. Clarinetist Buddy De Franco stands at left.

"Here artists have thirty to forty minutes to play; there you get thirty-two bars, twenty-six bars." Gillespie then cut his joking short, saying, "Before we can have an after-dinner speech, we've got to have some food," and introduced a Monterey-based band, Jake Stock and the Abalone Stompers. They swung into "Bourbon Street Parade," the first of several Dixieland jazz pieces the crowd would hear that night.

Billie Holiday appeared that first year, just nine months before she died. Wearing a fur to fend off the cold, she still looked like a lost little girl. Baritone saxophonist Gerry Mulligan put his arm around her and said, "It's all right, Billie; we're all here." And she started to sing "Good Morning Heartache." Not much was left of Lady Day's fine voice by this time, although it still gave you goose bumps, a voice that – with its unique phrasing –

held the crowd enthralled. "Travelin' Light" ("free as the breeze, no one but me*eee* and my mem-o-ries") was childlike, plaintive, poignant. Throughout the performance Holiday slurred her words. Finally, she was propped up and eased offstage by a host of loyal sidemen.

Dave Brubeck was thirty-eight at the time of his Monterey Jazz Festival appearance in 1958; Max Roach was thirty-three; Gerry Mulligan was the baby at thirty-one. Each of these musicians brought in a fine combo. Brubeck's quartet, with Paul Desmond on alto saxophone, was at the height of its prowess, its popularity already established by its "Jazz Goes to College" series. The group included Joe Morello on drums and "Senator" Eugene Wright on bass. At Monterey, on Sunday afternoon, they performed "Summersong" and

"G-Flat Theme" with the Monterey Jazz Festival Symphony, plus the pianist's brother, composer Howard Brubeck's "Dialogue for Quartet and Orchestra." The quartet alone played "Jazz Impressions of Eurasia," which employed the German, Polish and Turkish words for thank you as a rhythmic base: a compositional technique Brubeck still uses.

The Gerry Mulligan Quartet – Art Farmer on trumpet, Bill Crow on bass, Dave Bailey drums – offered "Festive Minor," a catchy light-tempo tune that successfully evoked the Festival's spirit. Gerry Mulligan, at thirty-one, was young and cocky and mildly sarcastic: characteristics he retained throughout his life. At Monterey, he said at the start, "I see we're practically assembled, for all practical purposes, yet I think we'll tune up first. By the way, Adrian Rollini is playing baritone for me tonight."

Not content with a handful of jazz aficionados, the Festival's organizers went out of their way to appeal to the public in general, even the uninitiated or "square." The 1958 program includes a definition of jazz taken from the *Encyclopaedia Britannica*, an article on the relationship of classical music to jazz, and a glossary, "The Argot of Jazz," which contained explanations of such words as "ax" ("any musical instrument, even a piano"), "charts" ("musical arrangement. See also Maps"), "finger popper" ("a cat [musician or hipster] who is swing-ing") and "far out" ("extremely advanced; gone . . . In music, modern jazz").

To the novice, some of the music presented at the first Monterey Jazz Festival must have seemed demanding or even daunting – as perhaps Mort Sahl's very topical humor did. The comedian was emcee on Sunday night. As popular in jazz clubs as the pianist he introduced, Sahl joked about Dave Brubeck's "wrought iron glasses." He made fun of an Ampex tape recorder that could actually answer the phone by itself. "Let the Russians top that!" Sahl exclaimed.

When Sahl introduced the Jimmy Giuffre Three (Giuffre plus Jim Hall and Bob Brookmeyer), he mentioned the fact that they traveled in a Volkswagen bus. Sahl mourned the decline of American cars with such names as the Chevy Agamemnon and Oldsmobile Oedipus. ("No headlights," he said of the latter.) The Giuffre group provided an original piece called the "Western Suite." The work was delightful in its artistry: an unusual blend of sound employing starts and cuts the way film does, with sudden shifts of tempo or mood.

The crowd responded resoundingly to the Max Roach Quintet with Booker Little on trumpet, George Coleman tenor sax, Ray Draper on tuba and Art Davis bass. On "La Villa," Coleman romped with rapid-fire lyricism. Roach's unaccompanied "Composition in Drums," just five minutes long, contained a

BOTTOM: The Dave Brubeck Quartet – Paul Desmond on alto sax, Brubeck on piano, Eugene Wright on bass and Joe Morello on drums – performed with the Monterey Symphony Orchestra. OPPOSITE: Harry James, an old friend of Jimmy Lyons from radio days, closed Sunday night in 1958. He and his popular big band would return in 1963 and 1965. After they played touch football with it backstage, James and Miles Davis walked on stage bearing Dizzy Gillespie's trumpet on a pillow.

history lesson in percussion, from initial rudiments to an explosive display of round-the-drum-kit pyrotechnics.

Looking back, the first Festival would seem to be a miracle of busy programming. That weekend also accommodated Rudy Salvini's Band from San Francisco, the Leroy Vinnegar Quartet, the Med Flory Band, the Mel Lewis-Bill Holman Quintet, Shelly Manne and His Men, Pete Rugolo conducting a combined Salvini-Flory band, Ernestine Anderson, the Cal Tjader Sextet with Mongo Santamaria, Dizzy Gillespie's Quintet, the Monterey Jazz Festival Symphony, with Gregory Millar conducting (presenting excerpts from Stravinsky, Hindemith and Milhaud), the Modern Jazz Quartet's premiere performance of Andre Hodier's "Around the Blues," John Lewis' "Midsommer," and Pete Phillips' "Toccata for Jazz Percussions and Orchestra," the latter featuring Max Roach.

On Sunday evening, closing night of the first Monterey Jazz Festival, the Dave Brubeck Quartet provided mostly jazz standards. "St. Louis Blues" contained classic Paul Desmond intervals, triplet stutters, and his overall fine tone. Brubeck offset this with percussive two-handed block chords and trills. Joe Morello had his day on "Sounds of the Loop," a riff tune that found the audience responding overtly to his smooth, no-nonsense, clean snare flutter and bass drum kicks. Harry James' orchestra appeared – along with Billie Holiday and the Giuffre Three – and that last evening ended with a jam session in which Benny Carter took just one solo chorus on the blues and the great Sonny Rollins sounded embarrassingly displeased and self-conscious on "I Want to Be Happy."

A miracle of programming that was largely slapdash and accidental, the first Monterey Jazz Festival had something special about it, something unique. The Festival had an international impact because it was part of an early movement – along with Norman Granz's Jazz at the Philharmonic concerts, the Dave Brubeck Quartet and the Modern Jazz Quartet, both of whom performed extensively on college campuses in the early Fifties – to take jazz out of the bars and night clubs. Like them, the Monterey Jazz Festival introduced the music to a wider audience, one that regarded jazz musicians as legitimate artists. Original Board of Directors member Sam Karas admits he was not a jazz lover in 1958. Nurtured on his hometown Chicago stereotypes, he thought of jazz

musicians as "cats" who played in smoke-filled sleazy clubs. At the first Festival he discovered they talked not only of music, but the eighty-four they'd shot on a golf course that day, their kids, or the new home they were finally able to purchase. They were fully human artists.

A musical first in the West, the Festival proved to be both serious and convivial, providing a wide range of talent. A host of musical styles existed side by side: the Dixieland or classic jazz revival, bebop, remnants of the big band swing era labeled mainstream, Third Stream commissioned works merging jazz with classical music, and cool or West Coast jazz. Who could ask for more? The audience would. They would demand it. They would ask for Festivals for decades.

BELOW: Baritone saxophonist Gerry Mulligan makes a friend on the Festival grounds. OPPOSITE: Max Roach adjusts the music for "Toccata for Jazz Percussions and Orchestra." Written by Peter Phillips, the piece was conceived for three drummers, and was, according to Roach today, "a lot of music." When studio commitments confined Shelly Manne to Los Angeles, and Joe Morello was unable to perform, Roach "did it myself, because, after he'd done all that work, I saw that look on Phillips' face."

TO JELL,
OR NOT TO JELL

Generally, the American Fifties is portrayed as a somewhat staid, complacent, conformist era (the "Eisenhower years"), but the image doesn't apply to the arts. Jack Kerouac's *On the Road* was first published in 1955; Allen Ginsberg's *Howl and Other Poems* in 1956. In the visual arena, Abstract Expressionism had come to fruition through the hands, and eyes of Willem de Kooning, Jackson Pollack, Robert Motherwell, Philip Guston and other artists. Stand-up comedy with a satirical edge was – thanks to Mort Sahl, Lenny Bruce, and Mike Nichols and Elaine May – enjoying a heyday. Allied with these other art forms, jazz music, too, had its pioneers, people willing to take risks, to go against the grain of the decade's complacency. As shown by the fare presented at the first Monterey Jazz Festival, a wide range of jazz styles existed at the close of the Fifties. Forty years after the first event, the great jazz artists who graced the Festival's Main Stage would – along with the writers, comedians and visual artists of that era – remain cultural icons.

Despite its legendary status today, the Festival evolved from humble origins. A suitable analogy is that of the mom-and-pop store. The Monterey Jazz Festival, at the start, was an ambitious yet home-grown, somewhat casual, even chaotic operation. The enterprise included a large number of family members. They all willingly and unselfishly pitched in to help out. Many would rise from humble status to positions of importance. Of the two founders, Jimmy Lyons and Ralph J. Gleason, one immediately became Festival general manager and eventually allowed his name to become almost syn-

ABOVE: In the Festival's early years, a mom-and-pop store ambience prevailed, volunteers arriving from all over the nation to offer their services. Penny Vieregge, left, wife of stage manager Paul Vieregge, and a friend worked on a set in an arena that by Festival time would be packed with animated, appreciative fans. OPPOSITE: Much in demand Los Angeles drummer Shelly Manne – who appeared at the first Festival with his own group, Shelly Manne and His Men – was one of a pool of excellent California-based musicians from which the first general manager, Jimmy Lyons, could draw. Twenty-five years later, Manne was still going strong and would return as part of the Festival's "house" band and become a familiar and popular figure.

ABOVE: Co-founder of the Monterey Jazz Festival with columnist Ralph J. Gleason, Jimmy Lyons held the position of first general manager, and held that post for thirty-five years. OPPOSITE: Co-founder Gleason, the nation's first syndicated jazz columnist (at the San Francisco Chronicle*) seems at home here in the Festival's press room, contemplating his next line, secure with his trademark pipe.*

onymous with the event itself. The other, while he would gain fame as an authority on not just jazz but pop, rock music and social issues, remained behind the scenes. He never acquired a formal title nor even an official capacity.

JIMMY LYONS: FOUNDER

"The radio man taught jazz: only/school that mattered more/than Jackie Quintana's dream rump..."– *John Detro, "Radio Man" (a poem for Jimmy Lyons)*

Although his late-night San Francisco "Discapades" radio show was a huge success, jazz deejay Jimmy Lyons grew dissatisfied with city life and, in 1953, fled south to Big Sur, an area known for its isolation and spectacular coastline. "This was the beginning," he said later, "of my hopeless love affair with the Monterey area." Born in China in 1916, the son of a missionary, having come of age dreaming of a radio career, Lyons served as the "Voice of the Orange Empire" on station KVOE in Santa Ana, California. He finally coupled a love of jazz and the mike by working as announcer for the

Stan Kenton Band. Drafted, he was assigned to Armed Forces Radio, where, for three years, he produced "Jubilee," a popular jazz program. He was the first jazz deejay to present such innovators as Dizzy Gillespie, Milt Jackson and Miles Davis on West Coast radio and he eventually acted as an advance man or publicist for Woody Herman, Gerry Mulligan, Chet Baker and Dave Brubeck. The latter credits Lyons with establishing his career. Established as a disk jockey in San Francisco, Lyons heard the pianist performing with an octet. Such a large group wouldn't fit into the KNBC radio studio, so Lyons featured a trio made up of Brubeck, Ron Crotty on bass and Cal Tjader on drums and vibes. By 1951, three of the trio's recordings were on *Metronome's* best-of-the-year list. Lyons himself was ambitious, a natural promoter, and so persuasive on the air that people such as poet/journalist John Detro regarded him as an early hero, a mentor who taught his radio audience "the difference between jazz pretenders and honest creators."

Yet Jimmy Lyons was a paradoxical per-

son. He could be reclusive, as evidenced by his sudden move – while in the forefront of the San Francisco jazz world – to the relative seclusion of Big Sur. Close friends and Festival staff members who served in the early years describe him as easygoing, affable, yet somewhat sedentary or cloistered. The Festival became his life. Board of Directors member Jim Costello recalls Lyons, camping out at the Costello family's Monterey home on the night his wife gave birth in 1956, avidly discussing his dream of starting an international jazz festival while "we all sat around waiting for the baby to happen."

RALPH GLEASON: FOUNDER

The writer grew up in New York state. At fifteen, Ralph Gleason found himself confined to bed with a bout of measles, listening endlessly to late-night jazz programs on the radio. He and Jimmy Lyons both attended Columbia University, but never met. Nor did Gleason graduate. Instead, he solicited newspapers around the country for the then unheard of position of jazz/pop reviewer. The *San Francisco Chronicle* bit, and Gleason became the nation's first syndicated jazz columnist. He was an intellectual with diverse taste, equally at home with music or the literary work of Nelson Algren. Astutely tuned to social trends and social causes, Gleason was reserved, a man who waited to be asked what he knew – which was considerable. He was also a diabetic who always carried a chocolate bar in his sport coat pocket. Gleason's warmth and keen humor invited the embrace, literally, of the sizeable singer, Jimmy Witherspoon. "Oh yeah, I really love Spoon," he would say, "but I wish he wouldn't hug me all the time. He keeps breaking my Hershey bar."

Gleason met Lyons in the late Forties, before the former worked at the *Chronicle*. Their shared passion for jazz resulted in a series of conversations focused – a few years before the experiment was actually carried out at Newport in 1954 – on the idea of an outdoor festival by the sea. According to Lyons, Gleason was the one who encouraged him to find a place "away from the sultry, dark, webby settings of clubs; to put music out in the open." The two had spent many evenings in such clubs, listening to and talking jazz. They even argued over the respective merits of pot and alcohol. Lighting up one night, Gleason asked, "Why do you drink so much?" Lyons replied, "Why do you smoke that stuff?" To which

Gleason responded, "Listen, you stick to your shit and I'll stick to mine." This, in many ways, defines the relationship. Lyons and Gleason. Yin and yang. More social critic than music critic perhaps, Gleason wanted the Festival to reflect what was happening in the world at large. Lyons wanted that world to stop and just listen to the music. In the opinion of people directly involved in the Festival's early days, Gleason was "a driving force," an "enormous influence" whom Lyons, in spite of his own sizable reputation as a jazz deejay, regarded as a mentor. Ernie Beyl, who served as publicity director for seventeen years, recalls that, once the Festival was established, he and Lyons would visit Gleason at his home in Berkeley, "without fail once a year," spending half the day listening to the critic expound on what should, or should not, be done at the event. At the start, Lyons followed through on these suggestions. The two men were different, yet they shared a vision of the event they planned.

"The Monterey Jazz Festival – or any real festival, jazz or otherwise – can't be just a collection of concerts. It must be a thing unto itself, an entity beyond the individual performances . . . The point of a festival is to be festive . . . the grounds, the concerts, the musicians, the patrons and the atmosphere all have to jell together to be something more than one can find elsewhere." *–Ralph Gleason*

BELOW: Paul Vieregge, left, who started work at the Festival in 1958, would serve as stage manager for thirty-four years. He is shown here with Jimmy Lyons, a friend from San Francisco television station days. OPPOSITE: At the start, the Festival pledged to present new and experimental artists such as saxophonist Ornette Coleman and pocket trumpeter Don Cherry. Musical director John Lewis had told Jimmy Lyons about the elevator operator in Los Angeles who played a white plastic saxophone and encouraged Lyons to book Coleman. Lewis predicted – correctly – that, given the future direction of jazz, "a lot is going to be coming out of him."

TOP: Darlene Chan was instrumental to the Festival's early success. Chan started out as an usher while a high school student and eventually became production coordinator. ABOVE: David Murray, left, was another key figure in the Festival's early mom-and-pop store days. He started out as a driver for performers and quickly became artist liaison. Since 1992 he has served as production coordinator. Murray is shown here with Dizzy Gillespie.

"A festival is an informal gathering of fans in a healthy setting . . . For our part, we've been trying to recreate the ancient European concept where there is a lot of everything offered the customer – outdoor entertainment between performances, refreshment booths, side attractions, everything, in fact, that contributes to a happy, holiday atmosphere."**–Jimmy Lyons**

Their language may differ, as did their respective personalities, but there was accord as far as purpose went. So much so that the separate statements might serve as translations of one another.

John Steinbeck had described Monterey's Cannery Row as "a poem, a stink, a grating noise, a quality of light, a tone, a habit, a nostalgia, a dream;" and, aside from the grating noise part, these words could well serve as a description of the festival that evolved. The official 1958 program, as if attempting to rival Steinbeck's effusive prose, characterized the Monterey Bay Peninsula as the grand lady of California, lively, wearing her past "with grace" but "consorting" with the arts and artists of the day and "having a ball doing it." Consorting with the arts and having a ball doing it was exactly what the founders had in mind. "The whole area was ripe for a festival at that time," claims bassist Percy Heath, who appeared with the Modern Jazz Quartet at the first Festival. Monterey was a beautiful part of the country, proximate to San Francisco where, according to Heath, a lively jazz scene was already in place, venues such as the Blackhawk nightclub flourishing. Jimmy Lyons had his heart set on presenting a festival in what he called nearby Monterey's "sylvan setting."

First vision, then implementation. Lyons organized a Board of Directors. Its first president was Monterey merchant Hal Hallett. Hallett and the Board secured sixty-seven one-hundred dollar loans from local business leaders and members of the professional community. Contributions were not just financial. Original Board member Sam Karas was managing a meat company back then. He allowed his panel trucks to carry combo instruments from the airport to the fairgrounds, and one large truck carted equipment for big bands. "We all had our assignments in those days," Karas reflects. Pianist Dave Brubeck recalls being invited to bring his quartet down from San Francisco to perform, or audition, for Monterey's city council in "a place that had whitewashed walls," per-

haps one of the fairground stables. When people ask Brubeck if he was present in 1958, he says yes, and adds, "We were the reason that the city council decided that it would be okay to have a festival in the first place." Official approval secured, the Festival was established as a non-profit, educational corporation.

Despite the impressive melange of musical talent assembled in 1958, for a cost of $41,000, all was not destined to jell at the start. When the newly established Board of Directors had its last meeting before the 1958 event, Ralph Gleason was present. The Board's discussion of the first Festival was ostensibly over and everyone started to get up when Gleason, sitting there with his pipe, said, "Gentlemen, I have one final question. What are you going to do when several thousand black people descend on Monterey, Pacific Grove and Carmel on a weekend?" Everybody sat right back down again, because, according to Grover Sales, who was there and served as Festival publicity director from 1958 to 1964, "in those days there were no black people in this area." The upshot of Gleason's question was: the Monterey Chamber of Commerce opened an office on the fairgrounds and a platoon of female volunteers called every motel, hotel, bed and breakfast and private rental residence in Monterey, Carmel and Pacific Grove, asking, "Do you have any objection to taking in black residents?" The response was as hoped. These volunteers were able to place every visitor in those areas, and there were no noticeably troublesome incidents.

THREE DISCIPLES

"There were very few of us doing a lot; it was too much, but we didn't know that then."
                                            –Darlene Chan

Looking back, Karas reflects, "The Festival belonged to *everybody*." At the start, it truly did. The mom-and-pop store analogy fits well, and so does another. The genesis and evolution of the Monterey Jazz Festival can also be compared to the inception of many organized religions. In this case, two visionaries teamed up with their shared dream, found an ideal site at which to implement it, and then gathered disciples willing to keep the faith and get the real job done. The initial stages of the institution were largely collective. Three disciples, key members of the faith and family, were Paul Vieregge, Darlene

Chan and David Murray.

Working at television station KRON in San Francisco, Paul Vieregge struck up an acquaintance with Lyons. Years later, when Lyons began to plan the Monterey Jazz Festival, he asked how he could get the sort of lighting Vieregge provided for his TV slots. Vieregge replied, "I guess you ask me and my buddy Milt Frankel to come down and do it for you." At the time, Lyons had already hired a stage manager for the first Festival, but an hour before show time, the guy pulled up a folding chair, sat down with his clipboard, and called out, "Mr. Gillespie, you're on first." Mr. Gillespie, unfortunately, was still back in his hotel room, so a compassionate Vieregge left lighting in the hands of his trusty friend Frankel and went over "to help this guy out, to see if we couldn't get things moving." After the Sunday night show, walking back to the office, Vieregge heard a smooth deejay's voice behind him say, "Well, I know one thing: I'm never going to do another

show without you as my stage manager." The voice belonged to Jimmy Lyons. The job would belong to Paul Vieregge for the next thirty-four years. A book and theater buff who wasn't into jazz, Vieregge discovered he didn't know one musician from another. He required the assistance of Vinnie Puleo, a former doorman at the Blackhawk in San Francisco. "Who's up next? Go get me Benny Carter," or "Get me Shelly Manne," Vieregge would cry, and Vinnie would respond, "He's standing next to you."

Ernie Beyl regards Vieregge as a visionary equal to Ralph Gleason and Jimmy Lyons. Beyl praises Vieregge's stage settings as "an organic element of the music," enshrouding performers in washes of light, dramatic yet subtle shadows that play off the stage flats like "grace notes to what the audience was hearing." Vieregge claims his crew was just concerned with allowing people at the far end of the arena to see what was happening on stage. Visionary or not, his job was to make the

ABOVE: Throughout its forty-year history, the Festival has drawn on a wealth of talent for informal jam sessions. Such events were exceptionally blessed in the early years. Here, trumpet master Dizzy Gillespie, left, and tenor sax giant Ben Webster, center, perform with three members of the great Duke Ellington orchestra: trombonist Lawrence Brown, alto saxophonist Johnny Hodges and baritone saxophonist Harry Carney.

ABOVE: Musicians loved the sylvan setting that Jimmy Lyons had selected as a site for the international jazz festival he and Ralph Gleason had dreamed of and discussed for years. Here, drummer Ed Blackwell and trumpeter Don Cherry kick back and luxuriate on the lawn: a favorite pastime for musicians and fans alike.

visions of others work, to implement their aspirations. He had to keep a total evening's effect in mind, making the sequence sound like one piece of music.

After the first year and word of the Festival's success got out, people came from all over the country to volunteer their services. The entire stage crew lived and slept in a Lone Oak Motel unit that housed a double bed in the front room, another in the bedroom, and plenty of space in the kitchen and living room for sleeping bags. Additional space, when needed, was provided by Volkswagen campers. Vieregge acquired what he calls "the world's most overqualified stage crew." This gang of artists, lighting designers and technicians, sound engineers, prop masters and grips included an internationally esteemed hydrologist named Cello Vitasovic, an aeronautical engineer, a book store and photo gallery owner, a geologist, and a computer consultant from Sao Paulo, Brazil. Many of them continue to return each year. Their dedication is typical of

the loyalty and continuity responsible for making the Monterey Jazz Festival the success it was and remains.

Referred to as "Jimmy's right hand," Darlene Chan was fifteen when she first attended the Monterey Jazz Festival. She went with some high school jazz band friends, and she literally caught on fire. This was back in the days when "people used to smoke a lot," and a man behind Chan put his cigarette out in her hair, or thought he had. When the fire flared, ushers rushed over and Chan remembers thinking, "That's cool: ushering." And safe. She served as an usher for about three years. Then, while she was a student at the University of California at Berkeley and organizing a jazz festival there, Lyons heard about her from Gleason. By 1966 she was working in the Festival office. As in the case of other grassroots volunteers, Chan swiftly rose from that position to production coordinator, a position she held until 1987.

"I was pretty good at organizing people

and getting 'the big picture' and they needed someone to do the jobs I liked to do," Chan says today. After performers had been booked, she and artist liaison David Murray conspired with stage manager Paul Vieregge to make things happen or work. Given the plethora of star performers that graced the Festival stage and the evolution of the event's appeal, Chan's job took on increased proportions. She was in charge of paying musicians, which made her very popular. Musicians wanted to come and play at Monterey. Half the time there were no contracts, that side of things taken care of by a telephone call or handshake. Booking itself was "pretty much Jimmy's show," Chan says. Those who had volunteered their services, or whom Chan calls "the family," discussed what worked and what didn't. Suggestions regarding innovative performers were listened to, if not always acted upon. Chan says that, because she was traveling, working for other festivals, young, exposed to a host of new trends in jazz, her recommendations may have carried the "kiss of death." A family joke was: if word got around that she *hadn't* thought of a particular group it might get on. But she says that Lyons' heart was in the right place, even if, later, his taste would grow increasingly conservative, even rigid, and the Festival would undergo what she calls "a sort of mid-life crisis" (what *San Francisco Examiner* jazz critic Philip Elwood labeled "a hardening of the format arteries"). Chan says, "I admired Jimmy Lyons. From the start, he was able to put on what he wanted and he stuck to his guns."

Chan left the Festival staff in 1987, but when she returns now, some people still think she's working there. "People still ask me: 'What time do I go on?' or 'Do I have my three amps up there?'" She still enjoys the family ambiance, the people, and she misses her peephole. Cognizant of her short stature, Vieregge created a special peephole for her, so she could see from backstage. "It had my name on it and nobody else could use it. I loved it. I felt so privileged because I was tiny and could never see." Her peephole was adjacent, stage left, to that of the man she occasionally returned to visit after she left the Festival's staff: Jimmy Lyons.

A high school dropout at seventeen and a devoted jazz fan who acted as artist liaison from 1961 until 1992, the year he became official production coordinator in place of Chan, David Murray is typical of many initial volun-

teers. His start was casual, nearly accidental. He hung out at the Blackhawk nightclub in San Francisco and ended up as doorman, checking IDs, even though he was underage at the time himself. That's where he met Lyons and initiated his thirty-six years of service with the Monterey Jazz Festival. Murray's duties evolved from escort service – supervising each artist's arrival, stay and departure – to hiring drivers, arranging rehearsal sites and renting backline equipment such as amps and extra musical instruments. "If someone needed a guitar string, I got it," Murray says. "Basically I was there to make sure everybody was happy."

These are just three of the many disciples or family members who shaped the Monterey Jazz Festival in its early days. The task of getting the event off the ground took all of them. Murray mentions Terry Cox, a highly successful maritime lawyer who started out as a driver and returns each year, even now, to serve in that humble capacity, asking no more. For such people, the Monterey Jazz Festival was both a sacred and secular event: a musical religion with a definite mission *and* a makeshift mom-and-pop store that had to stock and market its own goods. For years, the Festival has sustained both ends, but the road was long and not always easy.

BELOW: In 1959, Lambert, Hendricks and Ross served as emcees and created intros that described each performer in song. They would return in 1960 to perform in Jon Hendricks' "Evolution of the Blues Song."

MAINSTREAM,
THIRD STREAM and REACHING OUT

"We wanted the Festival to reflect what had happened to jazz throughout the year," explains John Lewis, who was musical director for twenty-six years. "We wanted the Festival to be a newsletter for the music in the United States of America." Mainstream and Third Stream music were again well represented at the Monterey Jazz Festival in 1959 and 1960. In accord with the times, the event also reached out. It expanded its range of offerings to include the highly innovative talents of Ornette Coleman, Eric Dolphy, the great John Coltrane and Elvin Jones.

The 1958 event had been, as Jimmy Lyons described it, "a real baptism of fire." It was tentatively organized, frantic, fumbling. It was exploratory surgery, even though packed with world class talent. Critic Dick Hadlock wrote that the affair was "immeasurably superior to Newport as a festive event," but only "slightly better musically." The problem was the same as Newport's: too many groups. After the 1958 Festival, Jimmy Lyons, Ralph Gleason and Grover Sales sought help and met for breakfast with pianist John Lewis, who was the esteemed leader of the Modern Jazz Quartet. They asked him to be musical consultant. When Lewis agreed, Monterey became the only jazz festival which, in Gleason's words, gave "the jazz musician himself a voice in the planning, preparation and programming." Yet Lewis' road was not easy. A few skeptical Board of Directors members, leery of experimentation, urged Lyons to hire commercially successful acts such as Dixieland trumpeter Al Hirt and pop singer Pat Suzuki as a sure thing, financially. The Board's devoted jazz contingent,

ABOVE: Trombonist-composer J.J. Johnson and Gunther Schuller look over the score for Johnson's highly acclaimed 1961 piece "Perceptions." OPPOSITE: The versatile jazz and blues singer Jimmy Witherspoon (shown here in 1976) survived a mid-Fifties career lull to become a sensation at the 1959 Monterey Jazz Festival, backed up by such jazz greats as Ben Webster, Coleman Hawkins, Woody Herman, Roy Eldridge and Earl "Fatha" Hines.

ABOVE: John Lewis, pianist and musical director of the Modern Jazz Quartet, confers with vibraphonist-pianist Victor Feldman of the Woody Herman band. In 1959, Lewis was named Festival "musical consultant," thus making Monterey the only jazz festival that, in Ralph Gleason's words, gave "the jazz musician himself a voice in the planning, preparation and programming" of the music. BELOW: In 1960, Gunther Schuller presented an afternoon of "New Music" that featured such jazz giants as tenor saxophonist John Coltrane, teamed with bassist Steve Davis and superb, perpetually smiling drummer Billy Higgins. OPPOSITE: The great J.J. Johnson, who astonished his peers with his fluid phrasing on passages once deemed impossible to play on trombone, proved himself an artful composer as well.

afraid that such obvious commercial choices would cheapen the event, prevailed. Faith in the fine taste and expertise of John Lewis won out. Lewis assured the Board that the public would come around. "It might take five years, but people will start coming to planned programs of original music."

It took far less than five years for Lewis' pledge to fulfill itself. The music offered in 1959 was extraordinary: a host of on-the-spot original creations arduously rehearsed. Lewis would show up with two dozen pre-sharpened pencils in a briefcase, anticipating changes to the score, and pass them out to the band. Trombonist J.J. Johnson affectionately complained, "John Lewis! John Lewis! You know what that means? Twenty-five rehearsals! Fifty-five hours of preparation!"

Lewis had some able assistance. In 1959, thirty-four-year-old Gunther Schuller, son of a New York Philharmonic violinist, showed up at Monterey. Schuller had performed on French horn with the American Ballet Theatre and Metropolitan Opera, and, in a jazz context, with Miles Davis on the influential "Birth of the Cool" session. Lecturing at Brandeis University in 1957, Schuller coined the term "Third Stream" to describe a form that combined elements of Western art music and jazz. At Monterey, he presented, and co-conducted with John Lewis, pieces for an ensemble half composed of musi-

cians from Woody Herman's Workshop Band and half from the San Francisco Symphony. The presentation disclosed, proudly, the results of its grueling rehearsal sessions and was thought by many to be the Festival's outstanding event. Not bad, considering that Earl Hines, Ben Webster, Coleman Hawkins, Ornette Coleman, Count Basie, Oscar Peterson and Sarah Vaughan were also on hand, making musical contributions.

Lewis' own contribution, "Three Little Feelings," began with a symphonically charged six note figure featuring J.J. Johnson's trombone offset by Conte Candoli's trumpet. Critic Gene Lees considered "Three Little Feelings" the best of the original compositions presented that afternoon: "a three-movement work of greater stature than its title would imply."

A full range of music was offered in 1959. Side by side with Third Stream stood rhythm and blues singer Jimmy Witherspoon, found living in Covington, Kentucky. When Jimmy Lyons discovered he was there, he called and said, "I want you at the Festival." Witherspoon replied, "Fine." When Lyons received no further word he called again, and was told, in true blues fashion, "I can't get there." Witherspoon had no car. Lyons sent him enough money for a used vehicle and the singer drove to Monterey for a triumphal session with Ben Webster, Coleman Hawkins,

Woody Herman, Roy Eldridge and Earl "Fatha" Hines. Hines had been called out of near obscurity, Lyons having found him confined to the Hangover Club in San Francisco. "What a terrible thing," the Festival's general manager thought. "Here's a guy once considered the first 'modern' jazz pianist, who teamed up with Louis Armstrong, the guy who discovered Dizzy, who discovered Billy Eckstine, now playing in a honky-tonk two-beat band." So he invited Hines to the Festival.

Witherspoon provided a blues set that people still rave about: his incomparable back-up band assisting with first-rate fill and solos on such tunes as "No Rollin' Blues" (which *rolls*!), "Good Rockin' Tonight" and "Ain't Nobody's Business." His phrases are succinct and humorous and poignant: "I like to love in the wee hours of the mornin'/When it's pourin' down rain" or "One day we got ham and bacon/Next day nothin' shakin'" and the classic:

> If fish can love in the water
> And worms can love underground;
> If rats can love in a garbage can,
> Woman, you better not turn me down.

Jimmy Witherspoon's mother, who was in the audience, had never heard him perform. A woman of strict religious principles, she would not go to clubs where liquor was served, not even to hear her son. But she heard him loud and clear at Monterey that day and the occasion concluded with a tearful meeting backstage.

Another hit in 1959 was guitarist Charlie Byrd. These early Festival years were fraught with budget concerns and when Woody Herman phoned Lyons and said, "I want to bring a guitar player with me," Lyons replied, "Woody, your contract doesn't call for a guitar player and we don't have the money for one." Herman shot back, "If I can't bring my guitar player I'm not coming." The object of contention turned out to be Byrd, who did show up with a unique small twenty-five-dollar amp. He wore a beat up leather jacket, struck an erect classical guitarist pose, and performed a show-stealing haunting version of "Mood Indigo." Also in the line-up was a rare encounter of mainstream saxophone giants Ben Webster and Coleman Hawkins with the avant-garde artist Ornette Coleman. Grover Sales comment-

ed that all the trio had to do was belch together and the event would have been considered history. Because of its range yet perfect blend of disparate talents, Lewis characterized the 1959 Monterey Jazz Festival as "only the best jazz festival ever held."

The Board drew up a statement of principles in 1960. It included the stipulation that the event would avoid "the hackneyed and the trite." The Festival would continue to explore "the new frontiers of jazz." At all cost it would avoid a parade of name acts unrelated to one another or to any significant developments in the music. Monterey hoped to place emphasis on original commissioned works and on uniting musicians who ordinarily didn't have the opportunity to perform together. Above all, the goal would be to make its artists feel at home and to create a unique and convivial atmosphere with respect for the music and the musicians at its core.

In keeping with these goals, the highlights of 1960 were two commissioned pieces: Jon Hendricks' "Evolution of the Blues Song" and Duke Ellington's "Suite Thursday." The much respected vocal trio Lambert, Hendricks

and Ross had served as ingenious emcees in 1959, providing the Festival with unity by way of spontaneously created introductions that described each performer in song. For "Evolution," Hendricks, who was a preacher's son, sat in a child's chair facing a group of children whose backs were to the audience. He told them the history of the blues, saying that "the spirituals are the mother of the blues and the blues are the mother of jazz." "They're hearing the truth now," trombonist J.J. Johnson commented backstage. Before the presentation was over, Hendricks had the Saturday afternoon crowd on its feet applauding, in tears as he was himself, backstage.

Everyone had been a bit nervous because Hendricks had no music to show the day before the Festival began. He put the piece together *at* the fairgrounds, sitting out on the lawn, producing what turned out to be an epic program. Jimmy Witherspoon, Big Miller, Odetta and Miriam Makeba shared in making it such a success. Hendricks came to consider "Evolution of the Blues" his statement, "the best thing I ever did." He feels the work dispels the lie that jazz started in houses of prostitution;

ABOVE: In a masterful 1959 combination, jazz giant Ben Webster, shown here alone, performed with saxophonists Coleman Hawkins and Ornette Coleman, the three backed up by the exciting Woody Herman band.

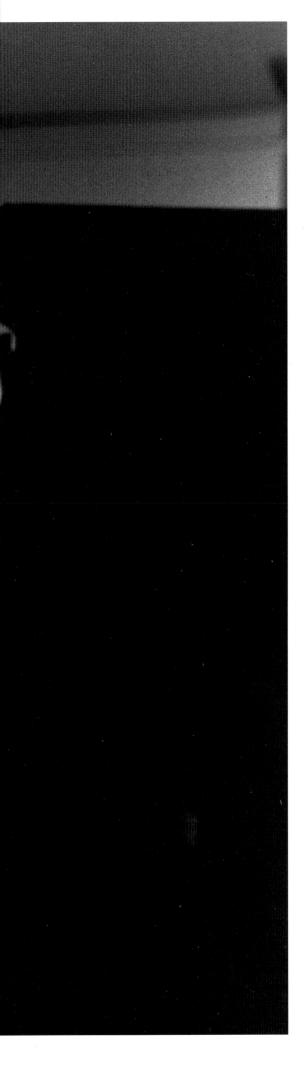

LEFT: Ralph Gleason cited Helen Humes' "electrifying opening chorus" on "Please Don't Talk About Me When I'm Gone" as one of the 1960 Festival's highlights. Like Jimmy Witherspoon, Humes was found back home in Kentucky, retired from singing, attending her aging parents and working in a munitions factory.

BOTTOM: Jon Hendricks' "Evolution of the Blues Song" featured the combined talents of Jimmy Witherspoon, popular folk singer Odetta, Miriam Makeba, and Big Miller, who is shown here assisted by tenor saxophonist Webster – bringing the blues to life.

OPPOSITE: One of the most popular, original, and musically rewarding artists to appear at the Monterey Jazz Festival was Count Basie, shown here at the piano.

ABOVE: In 1996, Jon Hendricks held a press conference during which he discussed the revival of "Evolution of the Blues."
BELOW: In 1961, following on the heels of his successful commissioned piece "Suite Thursday," Duke Ellington, right, was granted an open program called "Ellington Carte Blanche." He ended up playing mostly familiar fare made famous by such stellar sidemen as alto saxophonist Johnny Hodges, left.
OPPOSITE: In 1962, tenor saxophonist Stan Getz made his first Festival appearance. He is shown here with guitarist Jimmy Raney, left, and bassist Tommy Williams, right. Featured with his own quartet on Friday night, Getz also participated in a Saturday afternoon "Salute to the Sax" that found him in the excellent company of Benny Carter, Paul Desmond, James Moody, Phil Woods, Ben Webster, Bill Perkins and Gerry Mulligan.

citing American Negro church music as the real source of jazz – a music "America is at, but America doesn't know it yet." Why, originally, tell such a significant story to children? Because grownups destroy the true child, forcing him or her to live as we live: "lost, confused and dumb." Children are "much closer to where we came from." He wrote his history for children "because they would understand." Hendricks refers to Thelonious Monk, saying he was misunderstood because he was "a sensible six year old," and Hendricks himself, at seventy-five, claims he has succeeded in keeping the child in him alive, the "unborn spirit" that inhabits the body and gives it life. "So I'm seven. Well, maybe 7.5."

Duke Ellington's commissioned piece, "Suite Thursday," was originally intended to tell the story of another brand of innocents: the social misfits who inhabited Cannery Row in the novel by John Steinbeck. The work focuses on the romance between Row hero and all-around good guy Doc Ricketts and, as Ellington saw her, "a crude, proud little girl, kind of down on her luck," Suzy. Critics who recognized the

musical excellence of the finished product lamented its lack of relevance to the original tale, but jazz writer Stanley Dance doesn't agree. He shadowed Ellington through the arduous process of construction. Dance noted his "intense, brow-furrowed concentration," Ellington stepping from the shower to play a chord or phrase, or turning away from a TV shoot-em-up to try out an idea as soon as it occurred to him. The critic found the composition's "outward simplicity" in keeping with its subject matter. He praised the lack of pretension, "nothing highly colored or dramatic," and the fine use of contrasting movements (what a "suite" is all about), the orchestral colors reflecting the characters' own change of colors: a bum turns out to be a real angel after all. These two major commissioned performances were garnished with sets that included the André Previn Trio, vocalist Helen Humes, Cannonball Adderley, and returnees Gerry Mulligan (with full orchestra), Louis Armstrong, J.J. Johnson and Ornette Coleman – this time with his own quartet.

In 1961, Ellington was also granted a

program called "Ellington Carte Blanche," yet he played mostly his own familiar tunes. *San Francisco Examiner* critic Philip Elwood recalls Ellington sitting at a side stage piano, serving as emcee, loose, witty, offering "those wonderful phrases of his" while narrating "Pretty and the Wolf." A more ambitious achievement was J.J. Johnson's commissioned work "Perceptions," featuring Dizzy Gillespie, who appeared dressed in a black and white Nigerian gown, a beaded North African cap, and Yugoslavian leather shoes with up-turned tips. The opening was very *brass*, a fanfare amidst swooping harp and distant nearly Wagnerian intimations or calls. Gillespie presented themes laced with brass (four French horns, and trombones) and, when the soloist offered muted trumpet moods, two harps. A middle section pulled all the stops: flaring trumpet, backup brass, rare meters (6/4, 7/4), the work unfolding with stark dynamics: swift/sweet shifting to blaring assertion, into reflective decline. "Perceptions" was hailed by *Down Beat* critic Don DeMicheal as an "exceptional piece of work," Johnson among "the important jazz writers."

As if cloning himself for another victory, Gillespie was also featured artist on Lalo Schifrin's aptly entitled "Gillespiana." Gunther Schuller conducted the piece, which was written in a concerto grosso form. Gillespie moved elegantly and forcefully through its five sections, each representing a different phase of his music, and life. Of the non-commissioned offerings, Wes Montgomery, sitting in with John Coltrane's quartet featuring Eric Dolphy, seemed to be critics' choice on "Naima." Photographer Ray Avery recalls this as a "memorable session." Having run out of film during the middle of "My Favorite Things," he walked out to the distant parking lot to get more. When he got back Coltrane was still holding court on this extended tune. Original engrossing music and imaginative programming had paid off. The Monterey Jazz Festival, after just four years of existence, definitely stood out. Although jazz festivals were blossoming "like watermelons in the summertime," as Grover Sales put it, jazz critics Gene Lees, Dick Hadlock, Leonard Feather and Nat Hentoff found common ground in praising the Monterey Jazz Festival for its maturity, purposefulness, intelligent planning, friendliness, class, and dedication to the music rather than profit.

A major contributing factor was the relaxed atmosphere and unique setting that musicians had come to love, which encouraged solid respect for one another. In 1959, avant-garde or Third Stream advocates such as Ornette Coleman and Gunther Schuller, digging their music, clapped and egged on Chris Barber's classic jazz band. A sophisticated stylist such as John Lewis would listen to pianist Joe Sullivan's punishing stride on "Little Rock Getaway," and comment, "That's hard work." Sullivan had his chance to return a compliment later. A youthful Gerry Mulligan waltzed into a rehearsal and joined veterans Jack and Charlie Teagarden, and Pee Wee Russell. Mulligan took charge, helped pick out tunes, ordained solos, even though he'd never met these elder statesmen before. When Sullivan commenced his solid stride, the young baritone saxophonist said, "That old son-of-a-bitch can *play*;" and when Mulligan took his own solo, Sullivan expressed his appreciation by saying, "That Irish kid can *blow*!" If you could cut it on the bandstand, if you could play the music with the dedication and devotion it required, by 1961, no matter what style you played, all was equal on the Monterey Jazz Festival stage.

BELOW: In 1961, Dizzy Gillespie – dressed in a Nigerian gown, a beaded North African cap, and Yugoslavian leather shoes with up-turned tips – was featured soloist on J.J. Johnson's commissioned work "Perceptions."
OPPOSITE: Gillespie entertains fellow musicians backstage: Gunther Schuller (hand to ear) and trumpeter/violinist Ray Nance of the Duke Ellington Orchestra. Jimmy Lyons said he always wanted Dizzy to appear unannounced at Monterey on the back of an elephant, but the zany, zestful trumpeter was always riding on the back of an elephant, even with both feet – or as in this photograph, just one foot – on the ground.

DIZZY FOR PRESIDENT

THE REAL AMBASSADORS

Although the "crisis" was still a month away, thirty Russian ships had already landed their cargo of ballistic missiles in Cuba. Given persistent Cold War concerns, the theme of Dave Brubeck's commissioned piece "The Real Ambassadors," was daring for its day, yet simple. Jazz musicians were the *real* ambassadors of America: the best people to represent the best of *us* to the world. The notion was grounded in fact: Louis Armstrong, Dizzy Gillespie and Dave Brubeck himself had each completed extensive, highly successful overseas tours for the State Department. On closing night of the fifth annual Monterey Jazz Festival, in 1962, the first public performance of this rare, ambitious work was presented. "The Real Ambassadors" was a musical that featured the combined talents of Brubeck as composer and pianist, his wife Iola as librettist and narrator, and Louis Armstrong in the feature role. The piece also featured Carmen McRae, trombonist Trummy Young, pianist Billy Kyle, and the Lambert, Hendricks and Bavan vocal trio.

Armstrong was the ideal choice for the main role, even if he was reluctant to look the part. Asked to wear a tux with tails, striped formal trousers, vest and cravat and a diplomat's top hat, carrying an attache case, he refused. Yet Dave Brubeck recalls Louis' sudden stage appearance at dress rehearsal, sporting the prescribed costume, strolling past the pianist, saying, "Well, Pops, am I hammin' it up enough to suit you?" Both men broke up laughing, and "That's the way the play opened; that's how it began," Brubeck says.

In 1962, Armstrong's reputation extended well beyond the jazz world. Films such as

ABOVE: *The cast of "The Real Ambassadors": Louis Armstrong and Carmen McRae decked out in fur. OPPOSITE: In 1964 Gillespie would announce that he was running for President of the United States, and banners spelling out "Dizzy for President" were hung over the edge of the Festival stands. Here, the candidate smiles for his constituency. Jazz columnist and Festival co-founder Ralph Gleason (in sunglasses, with pipe) sits behind Gillespie.*

RIGHT: Dave Brubeck watches with appreciation as Louis Armstrong, in "The Real Ambassadors," responds to the line "Lift up the load and show us the way" with clear, classic jazz affirmation urged on by the refrain "Blow, Satchmo, blow forevermore." Because Armstrong was unfamiliar with the score, it was written out in extra-large notes. Lack of time prevented more than a single rehearsal at the St. Francis Hotel in San Francisco. "Broadway shows are tested for days, months, even years on the road," Brubeck reflects now, "but – pow! – we were right in it." At the time, Jimmy Lyons claimed "The Real Ambassadors" production was the most important thing the Festival had done.

*OPPOSITE: Tenor saxophon-
ist Arnett Cobb, on crutches
since a 1956 auto accident
that crushed his legs, looks on
as Dizzy Gillespie, in sus-
penders and beret, consults
with the perpetually impecca-
bly dressed John Lewis.*

High Society (1956) and *A Song is Born* (1948), hit tunes such as "Mack the Knife" and a 1956 CBS TV special "Satchmo the Great" made him a popular figure. His travels to Africa, Australia, Europe, the Far East and even behind the Iron Curtain had made an international celebrity of the former New Orleans Colored Waifs Home resident and alumnus of King Oliver's Creole Jazz Band. He had also appeared twice at the Monterey Jazz Festival: in 1958 and 1960, with his All-Stars.

Equally qualified as a "real ambassador" was Festival perennial Dizzy Gillespie. He spent time abroad when the State Department sponsored his 1956 big band tour of Iran, Lebanon, Syria, Pakistan, Turkey, Greece and Yugoslavia. This trip was so successful that musical excursions to Europe and South America (or what Dizzy jokingly referred to as "Alabama" and "Mississippi") followed. Gillespie was so innovative that his one-time boss, bandleader Cab Calloway, regarded his solos as "Chinese music." Gillespie and his helpmate Charlie Parker invented bebop, a form Louis Armstrong never learned to relish. Like Armstrong, Gillespie could maintain a supreme performance level and still make the music look like *fun*. When it came to the Monterey Jazz Festival, Dizzy acknowledged his role with historically-borne-out conceit, "It's assumed that I'm going to be in Monterey every year . . . I understand that the people expect to see me there." Indeed, if, as critic Gene Lees claimed, John Lewis was its "soul," Gunther Schuller its "brains," and Paul Vieregge its "muscle," Dizzy was its "glue," the very stuff – adorned in a beret, goatee and bop shades – that held the Festival together.

Gillespie was a Festival fixture for many years and the folklore that grew up around his behavior is extensive. When a young woman squeezed next to him at the Hunt Club VIP bar and cooed, "I've met you before, Mr. Gillespie," Dizzy replied, "Well, if you know me, kiss me." His quick quirky wit kept everybody on guard. He once leaned down into a restive audience, saying, "Now, cooool it, babee, else I'm gonna move next door to you!" He would introduce his bassist as "Christopher *White* . . . pardon the expression." Or he would introduce the whole band, to *each other*. "Christopher White, this is James Moody; James Moody, this is Kenny Barron." In 1964 Gillespie announced that he was running for President of the United States, and banners spelling out "Dizzy for President"

were hung over the edge of the Festival stands. Placards were made up, T-shirts embossed. The candidate's picture – taking the oath in top hat, tux and striped formal trousers – appeared on the cover of *Down Beat* magazine. He was going to live in the "Black House" and appoint Miles Davis Secretary of State. On stage, he would announce a "very short number," and, after a prolonged count off, blow a single note and stop. That was it. That was Dizzy. He could, like other exceptional people, go *too far*, cruelly distracting a young and nervous bass player during his solo with whispered obscenities, or offending both black and white at a late Sixties Festival breakfast with uncomfortable racial remarks.

Dave Brubeck – who directly honored Louis, and Dizzy by implication, in his 1962 musical production – was a real ambassador himself. In 1958, following in Gillespie's wake, Brubeck set out on a State Department tour of Turkey, Iran, Iraq, India, Pakistan, Sri Lanka, Afghanistan and, behind the Iron Curtain, Poland, Yugoslavia, Hungary and Romania. Travel inspired many fine performances, and some of his best compositions, including "Blue Rondo à la Turk." Dave Brubeck has always been one of the more uniquely creative figures in jazz. He was among the first to use two-voiced counterpoint exchanges (with alto saxophonist Paul Desmond), to employ unusual time signatures (5/4, 7/4, 9/4, 13/4), to play in more than one key simultaneously, and to include neoclassical elements such as atonality in his music. His strong hammering style served as a perfect foil, and guide, for Desmond's "cool" approach. Yet Brubeck wrote a classic tune called "In Your Own Sweet Way" and could play with tenderness too. He was a *complete* pianist/composer and was honored as such. Brubeck's face, against his choosing, preceded even that of Duke Ellington on the cover of *Time* magazine.

"The Real Ambassadors" embodied its theme. Louis Armstrong was *the* real ambassador: "All I do is play the blues/And meet the people face to face . . . I represent the human race." Iola Brubeck's lyrics were well-crafted, fetching, and occasionally biting: "When our neighbors call us vermin / We send out Woody Herman." They could be satirical (in "Remember Who You Are," at a briefing, diplomats are warned, "Stay away from issues") or sentimental in a manner that fit Armstrong's voice perfectly, just as "What a Wonderful World" would later.

"Summer Song," accompanied by Brubeck and Kyle on two pianos, is touching in its simplicity and truth: "Love to me is like a summer's day / Silent because there's just too much to say / Still and warm and peaceful . . . / Boats come drifting round the bend / Why must summer ever end?" Brubeck's score fit the purpose of each piece handsomely, and the message came through, whether secular – "Man, if they would only let me run things my way / The world would be a swingin' place" – or sacred: "He's watching all the time . . . If He cared if you're black or white / He'd mix one color, one just right. . . / lift up the load and show us the way."

Alas. "It was considered too controversial," Dave Brubeck remembers. After the Monterey performance, Broadway producers showed interest, but were afraid of direct public discussion, especially in a musical, that got near the subject of segregation and integration, in spite of all that was going on around them at the time. The Monterey production could have been televised, but wasn't. A crew was standing right there but wanted $750 to record the show, which was $750 more than Brubeck had on him at the time, or even in his bank account. Not to have that wonderful event televised remains "one of the biggest crimes" of Brubeck's musical existence.

Dave Brubeck has always been a good ambassador, reaching out to the world at large. His quartet recorded a tune called "Audrey," with its beautiful closing riff. The movie star, Audrey Hepburn, for whom the tune was written by Paul Desmond, told Brubeck she hummed the song's final refrain before falling asleep each night. When she died the pianist played the tune at a memorial service given for her at the United Nations. Brubeck's saxophonist at the time, Bobby Militello, copied each note of Desmond's solo and "Audrey" was performed in memory of its namesake. Brubeck was an equally active long-term ambassador at Monterey. He appeared at the Festival ten times from 1958 to 1992. As a Big Sur property owner, he – in the Festival's early days – had lots of contact with Jimmy Lyons. The two stayed up half the night talking about, as Brubeck puts it, "all those wonderful dreams about what could be done." These included, at one time, plans for a Brubeck ballet. The pianist feels that, because of the opportunity to perform such pieces as "Jazz Impressions of Eurasia" in 1958 and "The Real Ambassadors" in 1962, his Festival years were immensely exciting.

The ambassadorial, or international, spirit continued all weekend in 1962. Gillespie organized a presentation called "The Relatives of Jazz," honoring the influence of diverse nations on American music – Israel with singer Yaffa Yarkoni, Brazil with guitarist Bola Sete, and the Virgin Islands with its Steel Band. Lalo Schifrin's commissioned piece called "The New Continent" was international in scope, beginning with a movement called "The New Atlantis" and concluding with "Chorale." Billed as a "Divertimento for Jazz Trumpet and Orchestra in Six Movements," it featured – who else? Dizzy Gillespie. His trumpet surged and soared, right up through the work's momentous close.

A typical Festival embarrassment of riches, 1962 was fleshed out with Rex Stewart on trumpet and Earl "Fatha" Hines, Quincy Jones leading the Monterey Jazz Festival Orchestra, Vince Guaraldi's Trio and fine innovative pianist Ran Blake. Replacing John Lewis, who was on tour, Benny Carter served as musical director and prepared a commissioned piece, "Salute to the Sax," honoring Adolphe Sax, the Belgian inventor of that instrument. This work featured an outstanding line-up: Carter joined Paul Desmond, James Moody, Phil Woods, Stan Getz, Bill Perkins and Gerry Mulligan. Desmond and Mulligan provided smooth counterpoint on "Stardust," and agile phrases and delicious pauses on "All the Things You Are."

Even with all the good things offered, the 1962 Monterey Jazz Festival, with its host of musical good will ambassadors, could not prevent an unfortunate situation from arising, one that foreshadowed events of the late Sixties. A building strike halted work on the new 7000-seat Main Stage arena and non-paying "customers" milled around a makeshift pavilion set up 300 feet from the new site. A rowdy carnival atmosphere prevailed there, bongos and conga drums competing with the official musical programs. Teenagers jumped the fence, swinging from trees as if in a Tarzan movie. "Just too big a crush of people," says David Murray, who was actually pelted by rocks as he drove around in a golf cart. Fortunately, this presage of late Sixties excess didn't spill over into an actual riot, as it had at Newport. The disrupters were corralled and controlled. The incident paled beside the rich offerings of 1962, music that had truly reached out to the world. In this, the Festival's Age of Gold, not even the threat of a riot could compromise or curtail the Monterey Jazz Festival.

OPPOSITE: Louis Armstrong's pioneering State Department jazz tours made him the ideal choice for the starring role in "The Real Ambassadors." The audience loved this musical with a message: jazz musicians were, or should be, our genuine ambassadors! Hardened critics such as Ralph Gleason and Leonard Feather ("Who could be critical of me," Brubeck says today) were backstage with tears in their eyes. Even Armstrong was moved, and he was accustomed to melting hard hearts. In Africa, where he'd been treated like a king on his State Department tour, two warring tribes lay down their shields and swords long enough to attend one of his concerts, then went back to fighting again.

MONK, MILES and MINGUS

Three of the world's most respected jazz musicians appeared in Monterey twice each between the years 1963 and 1965. By the time of his first performance in 1963, Thelonious Sphere Monk was finally recognized as the original artist he was – a genuine creator who had succeeded, musically, in forging his own great good place. Miles Davis was a celebrity who'd fronted one of the greatest jazz combos ever (featuring John Coltrane on tenor saxophone) and whose collaborations with Gil Evans had produced such classic albums as *Miles Ahead* and *Sketches of Spain*. Charles Mingus was esteemed for his innovative bass work and for a long list of fine original compositions that included "Fables of Faubus," "Orange Was the Color of Her Dress, Then Blue Silk" and "Goodbye Pork Pie Hat." The mighty three were at the peak of their fame and the Monterey audience had been awaiting their arrival.

THELONIOUS MONK

Some early critics had dismissed Monk's complex wholly unique style as the result of ineptitude, of his being technically limited rather than pure genius, and he'd been forced to overpay his dues. Finally, after a decade of neglect (1945-1954) – not the first person whose highly individual vision had been equated with insanity – he was accepted as an original if eccentric icon in the jazz world.

He won the *Down Beat* Critics Poll in 1958-59, gave a highly successful Town Hall concert in New York in 1959, and appeared on the cover of *Time* magazine in 1964. Original pieces such as "'Round Midnight" and "Straight

ABOVE: Two giants of jazz converse: Thelonious Monk and Dizzy Gillespie. OPPOSITE: The musically restless, always questing Miles Davis appeared three times at the Festival, each time with a slightly different group. In 1963, he brought Herbie Hancock on piano and George Coleman on tenor saxophone. In 1964, Wayne Shorter replaced Coleman, and in 1969, Chick Corea was on piano, Dave Holland replaced Ron Carter on bass, and Jack DeJohnette replaced Tony Williams on drums. Whatever the group, the legendary Davis remained the same, providing inspirational leadership.

RIGHT: Thelonious Monk appeared at the Monterey Jazz Festival in 1963, but that appearance had been presaged by an earlier Blackhawk night-club date in San Francisco, where his reputation for erratic behavior preceded him. Contrary to expectations, it was Monk who showed up on time at the Blackhawk and the other members of his quartet who were late. When they did appear, tenor saxophonist Charlie Rouse displayed his mastery of what Grover Sales called "Monk's demanding repertoire." Sales wrote that drummer Frank Butler functioned as "Monk's third hand," and praised the pianist's own "raw slashing power" and the "harmonic daring of his massive chords." Everyone showed up on time at Monterey and the legendary Monk and his group didn't let the audience down.

No Chaser" marked him as one of the world's outstanding jazz composers. While it might take a few more years for people to acknowledge the absolute beauty of ballads such as "Ruby, My Dear" and "Ask Me Now," such pieces finally bore out his own wise advice: "Don't play what the public want. You play what *you* want and let the public pick up on what *you* doin' – even if it does take them fifteen, twenty years."

Monterey had been waiting for Monk, and Ralph Gleason called both the 1963 Saturday and Sunday afternoon performances "a total success." He commended the pianist's "mesmerizing style." In comparison, Monk's 1964 engagement was surprisingly subdued. On "Bright Mississippi," the tentative probing, the tenacious hesitations that make his style seem craggy, and the humor were all there. Monk himself said, "Anything that's good will make you laugh in admiration." Yet his solos were surprisingly tame. He didn't stab at the keys, his fingers like forks, as he'd been known to, but played spare Count Basie-like passages. His up-tempo solo on "Rhythm-A-Ning" was nearly deft rather than percussive – giving the lie to his technical limitations.

MILES DAVIS

By 1963, like Monk, Miles Davis was a long-awaited, much recognized master who'd been through many musical phases and paid a few dues of his own. Having grown up in an East St. Louis middle-class family, he attended Juilliard, but dropped out in favor of hanging out on New York's jazz-abundant 52nd Street. As a trumpeter, he established a reputation for his cool Harmon mute sound, pungent silences and parsimonious phrasing. Davis had a restless questing mind and was known for his continual and occasionally difficult growth as a musician. Not a trumpet virtuoso like his idol Dizzy Gillespie, he played his cool middle-range tone off against the more flamboyant styles of artists such as Coltrane and Charlie Parker. Constantly founding and reforming groups, he was what critic Scott Yanow has called "a brilliant talent scout." The list of players Davis discovered and showcased in his various groups reads like a Who's Who in jazz.

That first year, the quartet's late Friday night appearance was limited to a few numbers that, according to Gleason, displayed "sparkling virtuosity." Davis was featured in

duets with one of his most brilliant discoveries: the seventeen-year-old drummer Tony Williams. Next day, on his own, Williams teamed up with seventy-one-year-old "Pops" Foster, who was old enough to be Tony Williams' grandfather. They stole the crowd's heart, and Gleason hailed their duet as a "quiet demonstration of the unity of jazz and the timeless ability of jazzmen of all ages to swing together . . . a rare jazz moment." In 1964, saxophonist Wayne Shorter performed with Davis, and so well that many people forgot the heavy legacy of John Coltrane. Shorter's passion offset Miles' brooding tone. "Milestones" and "So What" were fiery tunes complemented by the compatible lyricism of the two on "My Funny Valentine."

CHARLES MINGUS

The last of this triad of jazz stars was bassist Charles Mingus. By 1964, Mingus had succeeded in fusing a wide variety of music: from gospel to Afro-Latin to symphonic. He explored every genre from songs to expanded suites, and each composition contained his individual stamp of rhythmic and tonal range, passion, complexity, and wild ambition. A composer of exceptional ability, he was also a man possessed of an occasionally maniacal temper, known for reprimanding or berating not only fellow performers but also, should their attention

BELOW: The charismatic trumpet master and brilliant talent scout Miles Davis finds a solitary moment on stage. OPPOSITE: Miles Davis' 1969 group included pianist Chick Corea and bassist Dave Holland. By this time, the trumpeter/leader, fascinated by the rock mystique, launched the jazz-rock-fusion movement that produced his influential albums In a Silent Way *and* Bitches Brew. *"What is this?", asked Festival usher Harry Crawford at the time. More people were drawn to Davis' new music than the arena could accommodate. When Crawford insisted that a man in an ankle-length leather coat take a seat, the gentleman suavely put a finger to his lips and uttered, "Shhh; it's Miles."*

ABOVE: Charles Mingus made his first performance at Monterey in 1964. Musician/educator Nick Williams, then a high school student, attended the two days of rehearsal that preceded the performance of "Meditations on Integration." Williams recalls Charles Mingus as "definitely the Leader," and that the bassist, who had a "stay out of my face look," pushed people around a lot." Young Williams worried about making the slightest noise and getting thrown out. OPPOSITE: Mingus' stunning, nerve-tingling presentation of "Meditations on Integration" in 1964 inspired prolonged applause not only from the audience, but from the musicians assembled backstage, who cheered as well.

fade or wander, audiences as well.

In the early Fifties, Mingus had been a member of Red Norvo's highly acclaimed trio, along with guitarist Tal Farlow. Mingus joined Charlie Parker, Dizzy Gillespie, Bud Powell and Max Roach for the celebrated 1953 concert in Toronto's Massey Hall. Something of a talent scout himself, by 1964 he had recorded his own compositions with a host of excellent musicians that included Eric Dolphy, Jackie McLean and Rahsaan Roland Kirk. The group he brought with him to the Monterey Jazz Festival was also tops: Charles McPherson on alto sax, John Handy on tenor, Lonnie Hillyer trumpet, Jackie Byard piano and Dannie Richmond drums.

For his first time out, Mingus offered a medley of Duke Ellington pieces, then one of his own, "Orange Was the Color of Her Dress, Then Blue Silk." Blues-studded piano turned impressionistic, then abruptly – "abruptly" being Mingus' stock and trade – converted to double-time trumpet and a driving rhythm, then back to slightly dissonant sax-led ensemble blues again. Yet all this fine music was merely a prelude to "Meditations on Integration." The mood of this piece was set by a union of Red Callender's tuba and Mingus' melancholic bowed bass. A slow heartbeat-obsessive rhythm takes hold, flute-laced, then sudden disruption; a soul-aching extended alto sax solo; an accretion of tempo followed by free horn passages with strong backing by Richmond and Mingus; a slow bluesy melodic portion with sudden cuts, fades, exaltations and expirations; dramatic staccato piano, horn transfusions over soft flute, bowed bass with its low-pitched sonority, a sassy trumpet joining flute and bass dialogue; then into a finale that found all instruments complaining, cajoling, cursing, converting into a wild rhythmic jailbreak that seemed to scale both heaven and hell, a fit of collective improvisation that ended with a trumpet screech, piano trill and sudden ensemble D-minor – the Monterey crowd itself going wild with whistling and prolonged applause, while Mingus embraced each of the performers and musicians backstage cheered. In reviews that followed, the piece was hailed as "nerve-tingling," "a tidal wave," "a blockbuster," "an essay in raw emotional intensity," "one of the great moments of Monterey music."

Many people vividly recall the Monterey appearances of these three musicians. First attending the festival as an usher, musician and educator Nick Williams saw Monk perform in 1963 and remembers that the pianist "didn't sit still for long." Offstage, the living legend turned out to be a taciturn man in an overcoat, scarf, hat and gloves – all of which he wore on stage, at least for a while. Removing these accessories, he played a few chords, re-dressed, literally changing hats, strolled and danced about, disappeared, and reappeared after saxophonist Charlie Rouse had exhausted his own solo. "I was lucky to be passing out programs and being that close to the band," Nick Williams recalls. Miles Davis was a different story. "You couldn't get near him. He was so distant."

One person, or at least his automobile, did. Writer Rick Carroll had the extra-musical adventure of parking his pearly white 1956 Porsche Speedster next to Miles Davis' blood red Ferrari, a thrill he still recalls – along with eating hot links and sweet potato pie that year, "with a very beautiful, older black woman who looked like Yma Sumac and turned out to be a clerk for Fredericks of Hollywood." Photojournalist Peter Breinig, the man responsible for first introducing Jimmy Lyons to Big Sur, claims the general manager was "scared to death" of the moody Davis. Lyons did, however, give the trumpeter the fanciest suite at the Carmel Highlands. Each year he appeared, Davis had a new car flown from New York to Monterey. In 1963 he got stopped by the police for speeding and never paid his ticket. When he returned in 1964, he was worried that the police might recognize him. "Don't worry," Breinig said, "last time you had a Maserati, but now you've got a Ferrari." To which Miles replied, "Yeah, but I got the same *face*."

Charles Mingus would follow his overwhelming 1964 success with a 1965 tantrum. Prior to this final appearance at the Festival, Mingus had unsuccessfully attempted to establish his independence as a producer as well as artist. When he arrived at the Festival he discovered that copies of *Mingus at Monterey*, a recording he'd made of the previous year's superlative performance, had not arrived on time to be sold in one of the fairgrounds' booths. Mingus blamed Lyons and was in a foul mood by the time he took the stage on Sunday. Halfway through a set called "New Music for Monterey," he told his octet to play "When the Saints Go Marching In" and marched the entire group offstage.

6

MORE GOLD

Whereas the giants – Monk, Miles and Mingus – may have seemed to monopolize the Festival between 1963 and 1965, they were by no means all of it. The embarrassment of riches that characterized the Monterey Jazz Festival from its start continued through 1965, the end of the event's Age of Gold. From 1963 through 1965 the event continued to reflect – as John Lewis hoped it would – all that happened to jazz throughout each year. A variety of styles continued to be represented: Classic jazz with the Teagarden family and Pee Wee Russell, mainstream music with Duke Ellington and Mary Lou Williams, bebop with the ubiquitous Dizzy Gillespie, and fresh younger talent as displayed by Horace Silver, the Denny Zeitlin Trio (with Charlie Haden on bass), and John Handy. In 1964, the first all blues show was presented on Saturday afternoon – a format that would prove so popular it's still in place today.

1963 is remembered as the year of the emotion-filled reunion of the Teagarden family. Brothers Jack on trombone, Charlie on trumpet and sister Norma on piano were joined by their mother, Helen, a ragtime pianist who jammed with her "children" on stage. "Considering the entire history of the Monterey Jazz Festival," jazz educator Herb Wong says, "that still stands as one of the most special events." An increasingly caustic Ralph Gleason remarked that the group occupied the stage for "an interminable length of time," but most writers and fans alike found the reunion to be the Festival's "most touching moment." Just months away from his own death, Jack Teagarden played and sang "A Hundred Years from Today."

ABOVE: *John Handy, who had appeared with the Charles Mingus Sextet in the stunning 1964 performance of "Meditations on Integration," returned with his own quintet in 1965 for an equally electrifying set featuring his own composition, "Spanish Lady." Handy was offered, and accepted, a contract from John Hammond of Columbia Records as soon as the group left the stage. OPPOSITE: Joe Henderson on tenor saxophone and Carmell Jones on trumpet played with pianist Horace Silver in 1964.*

OPPOSITE: One of the emotional highlights of the 1963 Festival was the reunion of the Teagarden family. Jack, Helen ("Mom"), Norma and Charlie all jammed together on the Main Stage.

1964: Based on the success of Jon Hendricks' "Evolution of the Blues Song," Jimmy Lyons invited the singer to put together a Saturday afternoon show featuring a full fare of that music called the mother of jazz. Hendricks responded with "The Blues – Right Now!" This program called upon the services of a long list of artists including Joe Williams, Big Joe Turner, "Big Mama" Willie Mae Thornton, and Homesick James. On stage, these artists made poetry out of an art form too often dismissed as a primitive precursor of jazz. Their crowd-stirring performances took the blues well beyond its familiar three chord harmonic structure, twelve bars and three line stanzas.

The great big band singer Joe Williams joined the Count Basie Orchestra in 1954, spent seven years there, and, with such songs as "Goin' to Chicago" and "Every Day I Have the Blues," acquired a reputation as a first-rate jazz singer. On "Every Day," although nobody loves him, Williams' powerful voice was not that of a victim but God answering Job out of the whirlwind: "Speaking of bad luck and trouble / Well you know I've had my share."

When he appeared, Big Joe Turner was a decade beyond his big hit, "Shake, Rattle and Roll," with its fine line: "I'm like a one-eyed cat peepin' in a seafood store." Yet the audience responded as if no time had passed at all. Turner gargled his syllables, with their earthy content, lending them a guttural, down home sound.

Take me pretty mama, dump me in your big brass bed;
Rock me till my face turns cherry red.

"Big Mama" Willie Mae Thornton would become a Festival favorite. In 1964 she cut loose on the song she made famous before Elvis Presley did, "You Ain't Nothin' But a Hound Dog." Signed to a five-year exclusive contract after Peacock Records' Don Robey heard her at the Eldorado Ballroom in Houston, Thornton recorded "Hound Dog," which quickly became number one for fourteen weeks on *Billboard's* rhythm and blues charts. Her version sold thousands, whereas Presley's cover version sold millions – as would Janis Joplin's cover of "Big Mama's" other hit, "Ball and Chain." Yet the Monterey audience recognized her for what she was: *the real thing,* an authentic blues singer. On "Hound Dog" her voice remained playful even while wailing, growling, wagging her tail, barking, bitching – all at the same time.

Homesick James had developed his unique bottleneck guitar style before he hoboed north from Tennessee to Chicago's South Side ghetto at the age of sixteen. A 1952 recording called "Homesick" earned him his name, along with a voice that ran words together like griefs, or was also capable of sudden full clear cries. On "Set a Date," he pleads, "Don't set it ta-ma-raw 'cause ta-ma-raw's too late!"

Evening Main Stage fare offered clarinetist Pee Wee Russell and an all-star group made up of such notables as Buck Clayton, Vic Dickenson, Bud Freeman and Red Callendar. Fine trumpeter Art Farmer made his first Festival appearance with his own group, as did Horace Silver. Jon Hendricks introduced the innovative pianist, claiming not many artists could play just their own compositions and "sound about as funky as you can get." Silver was ably assisted in this task by tenor saxophonist Joe Henderson, who blazed a solo trail that combined swing, stomp, funk and control. The familiar big bands of Woody Herman and Duke Ellington kept large ensemble standards high. The Festival upheld its reputation – one it had fought hard to establish – for rich and well-balanced programming.

1965 returned the spotlight to Dizzy. First he let his idolaters down when he said he would not run for President after all. He said he just didn't have the time. To ease the disappointment, Gillespie assisted his favorite arranger Gil Fuller in two premiered pieces: "Angel City Suite" and the appropriately entitled "On the Road to Monterey." The latter's "Big Sur" segment matched that coastline's rocky extravagance, and "17-Mile Drive," with its densely orchestrated Latin twist, showcased Bobby Hutcherson's expert vibes. On Sunday afternoon, a special called "Trumpets" teamed Dizzy, Clark Terry, Henry "Red" Allen and Rex Stewart. Voice of America's Willis Conover introduced the set, saying, "Jazz is not a *kind* of music at all; it's a way of playing *any* type of music – as many different ways as people playing it." The four men bore out this contention first with their varied tones, then their scat singing. That year, *New Yorker* jazz writer Whitney Balliett praised Buddy Rich's drum solo with the Harry James Orchestra as "breathtaking . . . whirling, ceaseless inventiveness . . . a mad, magnificent performance." And Earl "Fatha" Hines retained his many

LEFT: The great clarinetist Pee Wee Russell made two memorable appearances at the Festival. In 1963, he performed with Jack and Charlie Teagarden, pianist Joe Sullivan, and Gerry Mulligan. The latter improvised a blues duet with Russell that, according to Ralph Gleason, was more rewarding than performances by long established groups, noting it was "paradoxically delicate yet earthy . . . swinging along with the loping ease of a greyhound." Russell would return in 1964 with his own collection of all-stars: Buck Clayton, Vic Dickenson and Bud Freeman.

Festival fans, sounding more quirky-crafted, quixotic and inventive than Thelonious Monk himself.

Yet in spite of these highlights, 1965 belonged to John Handy and the premiere of the highly respected Mary Lou Williams' liturgical jazz work, *"Saint Martin de Porres."* Handy, who had appeared as a sideman with Charles Mingus in 1964, brought his own group: Terry Clarke on drums; Donald Thompson, bass; Michael White, violin; Jerry Hahn, guitar. Handy's original tune "Spanish Lady" opened with the evocative loops and swirls of his pure sax tone, its snake-charming sonority. Suddenly, shrapnel fragments of sax and a guitar vamp converged over a constant drum barrage. Sweet and sour, Michael White's violin clashed handsomely with Hahn's guitar, providing just the right tension. A gradual crescendo reminiscent of Ravel's "Bolero" led back to interlaced sax and violin. Then all stops were pulled for a closeout reminiscent of Mingus' "Meditations," displacing, momentarily in people's memories, the proud bassist. And "Spanish Lady" received a standing ovation.

This spectacular performance might never have taken place had it not been for the cunning of Festival publicity director Ernie Beyl. "I tried like hell to get Jimmy to go out to The Both/And Club in San Francisco to hear John Handy's group," Beyl says today. Finally, he invited Lyons and his wife Laurel out on a dinner date, one that just happened to find them in the vicinity of the club. When they walked in Handy was in the middle of "Spanish Lady." To the shock of his sidemen, he called the tune to a sudden halt, asked them to go back and begin again and, twenty minutes later – the audience erupting in applause – sauntered over to Lyon's table. "All right, all right," Lyons said, "you're going to play Monterey this year!"

The 1965 Monterey Jazz Festival reached a serene close with Williams' *"Saint Martin de Porres,"* a beautiful piece enlisting the aid of the Monterey Jazz Festival Singers. It commemorated the life of the seventeenth-century saint who was born, out of wedlock, to a Spanish father and an African mother. A brief blues piano vamp positioned the choir's intonations of St. Martin's attributes:

This man of love born of the flesh, yet of God
. . . to help the starving homeless . . .
black Christ of the Andes, come help us now
we pray.

In his review, Balliett praised the work but pointed out a condition that, unfortunately, would become a serious problem in succeeding years. He said the music was overlaid by "a smog of talk and laughter" on the part of a "chattering-guffawing audience." In spite of these intimations of a troubled future, the Festival was almost too good to be true: eight years of astute programming, a proliferation of exceptional talent, and festive cohesiveness largely unperturbed by incidents that, by 1965, had begun to plague the "outside" world. Yet a sense of foreboding tainted its free and easy, indisputably successful "vibes." As early as 1963, Ralph Gleason had noticed that the Festival's complacent or even dull moments were "more frequent than usual, the exciting moments fewer." He quoted Miles Davis' backstage remark: "You have to learn to close your ears and wait for the good things." Some fans began to grumble about the rut of familiarity, the mainstream cliquishness, the lack of fresh blood. Yet if these charges were true, the situation was about to change.

BELOW: The ubiquitous Dizzy Gillespie, musical consultant in 1965, observes the Festival's progress from his peephole backstage. This was also the year he announced he would not run for President of the United States after all, claiming that, while he was "very qualified . . . I don't have the time." OPPOSITE: At the 1965 Festival, Dizzy Gillespie's favorite arranger, Gil Fuller, premiered two pieces – "Angel City Suite" and the appropriately entitled "On the Road to Monterey." Fuller is shown here with vocalist Mary Stallings, who also performed that year.

7

ODD TIMES

Significant eras never seem to start on time. It's as if a decade has to wait a few years to realize exactly what it's got itself into. In this sense, the infamous Sixties was no exception. In Monterey the era started in 1966. Up to that time, the Festival was nearly monastic in its strict attention to the music and gave little indication – aside from the 1962 non-paying crowd's "unrest" – of much connection with the outside world.

Yet by 1966, the musical universe itself had changed. Two years before, the Beatles had displaced Bobby Vinton on the American hit parade with "I Want to Hold Your Hand." In 1964 also, Bob Dylan was singing "The Times They Are A-Changin," and they were. The Festival got raucously "relevant" by way of such non-jazz groups as Jefferson Airplane, Big Brother and the Holding Company (with Janis Joplin), and Sly and the Family Stone. But knee-jerking concessions to the era's trends were reflected in more subtle ways. One finds Woody Herman's orchestra (featuring a young Tom Harrell on trumpet) suddenly doing "MacArthur Park." They also had a go at "Aquarius" and "Light My Fire." Roberta Flack sang "On a Clear Day" and Leonard Cohen's "Suzanne;" Carmen McRae countered with the Beatles' "Something," Simon and Garfunkel's "The Sounds of Silence" and even the pop hit, "Elusive Butterfly of Love." Because these tunes had been hastily or half-heartedly embraced, the results were mixed.

As early as 1959, Ralph Gleason had written of future hopes that the Festival could expand its horizons and become a nine-day event incorporating all forms of contemporary

ABOVE: When Gil Evans directed the Monterey Jazz Festival All-Star Orchestra at the 1966 Festival, Cannonball Adderley, left, was soloist. The alto saxophonist also appeared with his quintet, featuring his brother Nat, center, and pianist Joe Zawinul, who wrote the group's popular piece "Mercy, Mercy, Mercy." OPPOSITE: Brazilian guitarist Bola Sete, with arranger Gil Evans standing behind him, rehearses on the Main Stage.

music. He did not implicate rock, then in its infancy, but an ardent fan of the music by 1966, Gleason secured its inclusion. (Three years later, Gleason's book, *The Jefferson Airplane and the San Francisco Sound*, would contain a classic assessment of the rock scene.) The Count Basie Orchestra performed shoulder to shoulder with Jefferson Airplane, with room left over for the advanced, sophisticated charts of Gil Evans and a taste of funk provided by Cannonball Adderley and Joe Zawinul doing "Mercy, Mercy, Mercy."

The most private of revolutionaries, by the time he turned up at Monterey in 1966, Gil Evans was acclaimed for his pioneering work with the Claude Thornhill Orchestra and his handsome and far-sighted arrangements for Miles Davis' *Miles Ahead*, *Porgy and Bess* and *Sketches of Spain* albums. Evans was inventing a musical future filled with dark moody polyphony and advanced harmony. A perfectionist, his appearances were rare. "The first time I've done anything with a band in public in years!" he told Gleason. "It's hard to find the right players." But, awaiting Evans' arrival, bassist Ray Brown found them, and rehearsed a band in Los Angeles. At the 1966 Festival, Evans' arrangement of Jelly Roll Morton's "King Porter Stomp" resembled previous versions only in the parodic riffs set behind Cannonball Adderley's up-tempo romp. An Evans' original "Barracuda," was ominous, filled with a rich new blend of timbres and the predatorial insistence of the section work.

The tenth anniversary Monterey Jazz Festival, in 1967, commenced with the, literally, odd times of Don Ellis: 32/8, 15/16, and on "Pussy Wiggle Stomp," a sudden change from 17/4 to 14/4. This was the full cry music of a not-so-gentle revolutionary. Ellis pioneered his four-valve trumpet: an amplified horn that, using microtones, provided twenty-four notes per octave, plus reverb. His big band included three basses, a reed section boasting three soprano saxophones, amplified flutes, and, on a tune called "Turkish Bath" – in keeping with the times – three sets of drums and an amplified sitar. And, as if the overdose of *sound* weren't enough, the Festival went all out to celebrate its first decade by releasing clusters of brightly colored balloons while blinding white spotlights blinked on and off on each side of the stage.

Ornette Coleman, decked out in a gold-embroidered black silk suit, fronted a new quartet with the remarkable Charlie Haden on bass. They played "Haight-Ashbury." *Newsweek* magazine smugly reported that a few "grossly outnumbered hippies tinkled along with beads and bells." Gill Melle and his Electronic Jazz Quartet offered a demonstration of computers, light cues and feedback devices. Experiencing such a polyglot menu, observers must have found it difficult to tell just where, after ten successful years, the Festival was headed, or just what portion of the audience was being catered to.

By 1968, the world at large was boiling over, but not the Monterey Jazz Festival, which suffered one of its tamest, most uninspired programs in years. "Outside" the Festival, Martin Luther King was assassinated. Social critic Benjamin DeMott commented on the "uncommon vulgarity and tastelessness" he felt had taken hold of the nation in everything from statements that "God is dead" to H. Rap Brown's "How many white folks have you killed today?" Summers had become open season for burnings, lootings, assaults and mass arrest. Vietnam had divided and radicalized Americans like no other event since the Civil War.

To those who made up the twenty-six thousand paid admissions in 1968, the Monterey Jazz Festival might have seemed like an oasis of sanity in a world gone mad. A "Generation of Vibers" featured solo appearances by five first-rate vibraphonists: Gary Burton, Bobby Hutcherson, Cal Tjader, Milt Jackson and Red Norvo; no one musician upstaging the others. To critic Leonard Feather, this event was "the most perfectly conceived and executed" of the Festival's sets. Lalo Schifrin returned to conduct his "Jazz Suite on the Mass Texts" featuring an eighteen-piece choir, a piece regrettably juxtaposed, in Feather's view, with the appearance of Earl "Fatha" Hines' dancing teenage daughter. With the fairgrounds seventy-five percent empty on a Sunday night, it was "a dismal ending to one of the most forgettable Festivals in Monterey's generally distinguished history."

This eleventh annual Monterey Jazz Festival was also plagued by severe sound problems, a situation for which president of the Board Mel Isenberger apologized, promising "the best sound that can be provided by audio technology" for the following year. But critics had begun to focus on larger issues. The esteemed Leonard Feather wrote that, at first glance, because of the multitude of fairgrounds concessions and apparent trouble-free frater-

nization between the races, the Festival seemed "mercifully transplanted away from the national nightmare," but a closer look, he continued, revealed stark polarization even in the "supposedly enlightened world of jazz." Now, even the Festival's legendary good will was being called into question.

After the 1969 event, Langdon Winner, a music critic for *Rolling Stone* (with its, admittedly, rock bias), went so far as to sound the death knell in an article entitled "Monterey Jazz: A Festival No More." He faulted the occasion for its "pervasive hollowness," and asserted that performers and audiences have rarely been "so strangely alienated from each other." Yet the twelfth annual Monterey Jazz Festival contained some fine fresh musical offerings. Miles Davis returned with twenty-eight-year-old Chick Corea (on electric piano) in tow, and drummer Jack DeJohnette. The Davis group, which also included Wayne Shorter and the excellent bassist Dave Holland, was itself stretching out, basing their improvisations on arbitrary scales and/or modes, "rendering all conventional frames of reference obsolete," according to *Down Beat's* Harvey Siders. "Old" drummer Tony Williams, who was all of twenty-four by now, brought his own group, Lifetime. Winner hailed them, probably because the group included British rock guitarist John McLaughlin and an exciting young organist, Larry Young, who provided "some of the most intense and truly weird music in jazz right now."

These *were* odd times. Even Third Stream music, far less prominent than it had

ABOVE: In a 1967 reincarnation of Third Stream music, Yugoslavian composer Miljenko Prohaska's "Dilemma" was a "striking and expertly crafted piece of music," according to critic Dan Morgenstern. Alto saxophonist James Moody played such stunning flute that fellow musicians stood up and applauded. Moody, left, is shown here in a 1962 Festival performance with Quincy Jones. OPPOSITE: Charles Lloyd, who would go on to charm audiences at Bill Graham's San Francisco rock pavilion, the Fillmore West, brought a quartet featuring a flamboyant twenty-one year old pianist named Keith Jarrett, along with an equally ebullient drummer, Jack DeJohnette. Lloyd, a superb reed player, would retire briefly from jazz to become a teacher of transcendental meditation. He would not return to the Festival again until 1993, twenty-seven years after his legendary Forest Flower album, recorded at the Festival in 1966, sold over one million copies.

been in the Festival's early years, reared its head again. Sunday's concert opened with John Lewis' "Strings at Monterey," a "civilized surprise" according to Siders, who felt the program showed as much courage, given the new trends in music, as fine musicianship on the part of Lewis. Variations on Bach's "Air on a G-String" and an adaption of Purcell's "Dido's Lament" were presented alongside the pianist's own "Vendomne," along with an original work by Bill Fischer ironically entitled "Rise and Fall of the Third Stream." In contrast, the Buddy Rich big band put in what critic Siders felt was "an outstanding set" with Rich, never short on ego, kicking off each and every number (the "Me Decade" waiting in the wings) with a drum cadenza.

The bouillabaisse programming continued on into the Seventies, that new decade that John Lennon said he slept through. Nostalgia was most blatantly represented at Monterey in 1970 by the team of Slim and Slam (guitarist Slim Gaillard and bassist Slam Stewart), their once-hip 1940s phrases, such as "mellowroonie" and "macvoutie," perhaps puzzling to younger members of the audience. Attempting to be very much "with it," Duke Ellington's Orchestra premiered an entirely new suite, "The Afro-Eurasian Eclipse," based on the fashionable "the medium is the message" concept of Marshall McLuhan. The communications expert not only saw the medium as more influential than the content, but viewed the world as a "global village," becoming increasingly integrated through modern technology. However, Duke's introduction showed his haste to skip over McLuhan's theorizing and get to the music itself. "The whole world's going Oriental, nobody can retain their identity," Ellington said, "very intellectual and all that . . . roll it, man!" What the band rolled, after a fairly dissonant opening replete with heavy "doomsday" accents and uncustomary "Far East" voicings, was a pleasant and occasionally exciting pastiche of rich orchestral color with no apparent unifying theme.

The 1970 Monterey Jazz Festival again made an effort to provide new sounds and faces: the low-key quintet of flutist Tim Weisberg; fine pianist Hampton Hawes with a trio that included bassist Leroy Vinnegar (who'd been present with his own group at the first Festival in 1958), and a reunion of legendary saxophone veterans Sonny Stitt and Gene Ammons. Fleshed out with more Third Stream offerings and the Johnny Otis Blues Show, diverse, inconsistent, harkening back to the expansiveness of its first days and nights, the Festival was surviving its own, and the nation's, growing pains; its reputation fairly well intact.

In 1971 Louis Armstrong died. That year's event was suitably dedicated to one of its genuine heroes. A southern California nursery named Armstrong provided rows and rows of a new rose, a creation named "Jazz Fest," that were set in front of the Main Stage. A host of fine trumpeters were on hand. Friday night started with Clark Terry playing "Misty," and

Roy Eldridge "Willow Weep for Me." On Saturday night, Thad Jones, Dizzy Gillespie, Terry, Eldridge and Chuck Findley paid another trumpet tribute to "Pops."

That Festival closed with a homage to Norman Grantz's Jazz at the Philharmonic, whose spontaneous concerts had served as a model for Jimmy Lyons. The Sunday evening jam session included former JATP stars Roy Eldridge, Bill Harris, Eddie "Lockjaw" Davis, Zoot Sims, Louis Hayes and Oscar Peterson – an event that left *Down Beat* critic Siders "basking in the afterglow." Citing recent criti- cism of Lyons' preference, year upon year, for the same personal favorite performers, Siders said that was the general manager's preroga- tive. "It's *his* festival and he can do with it as he sees fit," the critic wrote. But others were not so kind, nor charitable.

Original co-founder Ralph Gleason took on the role of Festival conscience, and he was severe. In a 1971 article called "Sour Notes at the Jazz Festival," the *Chronicle's* critic attacked the excessive drinking, an audience "awash in a sea of booze." In his eyes, the Festival had become a "three-day, free-form

bash which has increasingly degenerated into little to do with actual music." He mourned the lack, or loss, of innovation, claiming that "gimmickery" had been substituted in its place. Monterey was no longer "the realization of a dream," but had succumbed to programming so safe, so careful, so stingy that there was no room for anything "but an occasional good performance."

In a 1971 *Los Angeles Times* column, Leonard Feather wrote "An open letter to a jazz impresario," congratulating Lyons on a fourteenth annual Festival which ran its course "happily, without the slightest sign of trouble." Then, mentioning the ten-foot-high iron gates topped with barbed wire set against these "turbulent times," the critic accused Lyons of a preoccupation with mere personal and professional "survival." Feather pointed out the generation gap that was widening (in 1971, John Handy, at thirty-eight, was the youngest of the "name" group leaders heard), mentioned exciting young performers such as Freddie Hubbard and Herbie Hancock, neither of whom were invited to the Festival. Feather faulted Lyons for *not* telling "the whole story" of what was happening in the jazz world of the day, and expressed hope that the following year's allocation of time would be "pro-rated just a little more substantially in favor of the *present*."

Looking back at those years with perspective, *San Francisco Examiner* critic Philip Elwood says that, by the end of the Sixties, Festival management found its original 1960-stated artistic principles too "high-minded" in light of its financial and historical realities. The Monterey Jazz Festival could no longer portray itself as the "American Salzburg" critics and musicians once dubbed it. As Gleason grew more impatient with imperfection, Lyons was selling tickets and giving an audience he would increasingly regard as "family" exactly what they wanted by way of music.

In 1971, Lyons responded to the charges of critics such as Gleason and Feather in two ways. First, after consulting with musical director John Lewis, he invited Herbie Hancock to the 1972 Monterey Jazz Festival. But then, at the event, disturbed by forty-five minutes of what he considered "noodling avant-garde," Lyons told Paul Vieregge to close the curtain on Hancock, before the end of his piece. He also put Sonny Rollins on the bill. Lyons' second response, faced with this sudden clamor for the "new," was to fall back on inexorable

business logic: you can't argue successfully against *success*.

Indeed. The 1972 Monterey Jazz Festival drew 32,300 fans who paid $170,000 for a three-day, five-concert "bash." About 1,750 of them settled for a closed-circuit TV experience of the event, shown in a fairgrounds barn. Lyons took pride in the quantity as well as the quality of his followers, citing young doctors and lawyers, affluent black and white professional people as among the first to order tickets each year. He even saluted the impecunious who salted away quarters in a jar, cashing them in at the bank in April in order to cover admission. Lyons talked about visitors (as distant as Fresno and Milwaukee) who'd met by chance as seatmates, and become fast once-a-year friends, now exchanging Christmas presents. In his review of the 1972 Festival, Feather recanted his charges of the previous year somewhat. He referred to the "virtually unbreakable bond of jazz" that lay at the core of the Festival's success, along with what the critic now acknowledged as "frequent musical surprises." Feather admitted that neither "social upheaval" nor "musical revolution" could forestall Monterey from "pushing on toward its silver jubilee." And the Festival – having survived so much of what had been placed in its way – did just that.

BELOW: In 1967, drummer Louie Bellson provided two orginal compositions that were presented by the Don Ellis Orchestra: "Sketches" and "Memorial to Billy Strayhorn." Bellson also performed with Illinois Jacquet's quartet that year, and in 1971 appeared with his own All-Star Band, which included Harry "Sweets" Edison, Joe Pass and Ray Brown. OPPOSITE: In 1965, the esteemed New Yorker *jazz writer Whitney Balliett, making his first Festival visit, praised Buddy Rich's drum solo with the Harry James Orchestra as "breathtaking . . . whirling, ceaseless inventiveness . . . a mad, magnificent performance."*

THE ROCK INVASION

In a 1967 article called "Like a Rolling Stone," Ralph Gleason claimed that for a true sense of what was happening in America, one must turn not to jazz but to "rock 'n roll, to popular music" – citing Buffalo Springfield's stark lyrics: "STOP, children, what's that sound? Everybody look what's goin' down." One year earlier, Jimmy Lyons, acknowledging the times and urged on by Gleason, added a fresh element to the Saturday afternoon blues show: the rock invasion. Six years later, Lyons would admit he'd learned a lesson when he "submitted to pressure" to include rock groups, that more jazz patrons were "alienated than attracted," yet he also expressed pride at being the first person to present – before the 1967 Monterey Pop Festival – such groups as Jefferson Airplane, and Big Brother and the Holding Company featuring Janis Joplin.

The 1966 invasion got under way with a fairly classy rock-oriented white blues group from Chicago: the Paul Butterfield Blues Band, with twenty-three-year-old Mike Bloomfield on electric guitar. Bloomfield would go on to make a name for himself with the rock group Electric Flag and with *Super Session*, a recording of jam sessions with Al Kooper and Stephen Stills. This, plus his work aside Bob Dylan, helped establish the blues guitarist as a magical figure. Butterfield's band had an unaffected, authoritative modern urban blues voice of its own, and could truly *swing* while meeting the fundamental rock requirement of uncompromised volume.

It is not at all difficult to imagine a woman like the raucously effervescent Dee Dee Rainbow initiating her gestic revels in 1966,

leading her dancing troops up and down Main Stage aisles in cadence with Paul Butterfield's blistering music. Nor is it difficult to imagine them doing the same in time with Jefferson Airplane, even in its pre-Grace Slick, pre-"White Rabbit" phase. Jefferson Airplane was just a year (and Grace Slick) away from its first big national hit, "Somebody to Love," yet already represented an era of Flower Power, the Diggers, and a Gathering of the Tribes or Human Be-In that attracted twenty-thousand people to Golden Gate Park just four months after the Airplane's appearance in Monterey.

By the following year, the Festival crowd was dancing in the aisles to the raucous music of Big Brother and the Holding Company, and its astonishing vocalist, Janis Joplin. Yet not everyone was favorably impressed with the singer who would become a legend in her own time. Willis Conover called Joplin "an uncured ham" and found her musical associates "heavy and relentlessly unswinging." Jazz authority Dan Morgenstern wrote that Joplin was "a bit strained in her efforts to sound authentic" and the amplification "monumentally loud." What impressed him was the "happy sight" of so many people "snaking up and down the aisles," others standing on their chairs gyrating in time to the hand-clapped encouragement and cries of the rest of the audience.

Other attempts on the part of Festival management to expand the musical offerings resulted in the appearance of vocalist/guitarist Richie Havens, who critic Morgenstern found "an interesting performer . . . sincere and affecting." Yet in a 1972 interview with Leonard Feather, Lyons asserted there were plenty of

OPPOSITE: Writer Rick Carroll claims he will never forget the afternoon in 1967 when his high school pal-turned-guitar player, Sam Andrew, left, walked out on stage as part of a group – Big Brother & the Holding Company – that would back up a "new, blue-eyed frizzy-haired singer named Janis Joplin." After Joplin finished the set and blew her nose on the Main Stage curtain, the group walked off "higher than kites." Joplin knew she knocked the Saturday afternoon crowd dead. "The bloods dug it," she kept saying, "the bloods dug it." Then she climbed into her blue Hillman Minx "stuffed with junk food wrappers," according to Carroll, and drove off to "her ultimate fame as a legend in her own time."

BELOW: The rock and raucous blues spirit that enlivened the mid-Sixties was still going strong in 1973, when Bo Diddley made his first Festival appearance with his box-shaped guitar. He would return in 1974 and 1983, and the crowd would still be dancing.

OPPOSITE TOP: One phenomenon none of the Festival founders foresaw back in 1958 was the descent, from Seattle, of a woman whose presence has become synonymous with the event's festive spirit. Dee Dee Rainbow, or the Rainbow Lady, is shown here in her effusively colorful garb: her face flecked with gold dust, decked out in feather boas, rings ranging from turquoise Navajo to cast silver Chinese dragons, carrying her full-spectrum umbrella and a wondrous wand that resembles the globe, a fully lit fountain, and a fireworks display. Each year, Dee Dee Rainbow leads a Saturday afternoon parade she inaugurated in the mid-Sixties, her motto inscribed on a badge that reads, "Enjoy life: this is not a dress rehearsal."

OPPOSITE BOTTOM: On Saturday afternoons in the Sixties, the Festival arena would explode. Occasionally a sodden-but-athletic spectator would dance atop the balance beam of a rail in the stands. His upper body undulating in time to the music, he sauntered from section to section, precariously perched, much to the delight of the cheering crowd. On Saturday afternoon the audience was not at all surprised by the sight of a topless woman or lovers who would abandon the privacy of sleeping bags, displaying their art form in the stands.

opportunities for rock artists to be heard in concert "among their own audiences." The line between such groups and "honest jazz players" had been drawn, although Lyons would succumb to temptation once again in 1975, when he asked Blood, Sweat and Tears to perform, a group that augmented the traditional rock quartet with a four-man horn section. Although vocalist David Clayton-Thomas paid homage to Cannonball Adderley, who died just a month earlier (and whom none of the jazz participants saw fit to honor all weekend), critics were not impressed by Blood, Sweat and Tears' attempted marriage of jazz and rock. The audience, however, remained on its feet in appreciation for the entire set.

Did the Monterey Jazz Festival get as wild, permissive, indulgent as the Sixties stereotype suggests? The answer from sources present is an unqualified, "Yes." The words they use to describe those nights and days are: "Wonderful!" "Dynamic!" "Mostly good fun!" "Very special." "The best party ever thrown!" Jimmy Lyons, Ralph Gleason and John Lewis had all stressed the importance of the event's "festive" side and, linked to an era governed by the maxim "If it feels good, do it!", they probably got far more than they'd bargained for.

"Police Force Is Beefed Up, And Merchants, Motel Men Expect More Than Music" was the subtitle of a 1968 *Wall Street Journal* article on the Festival. Economic optimism was coupled with civic misgiving. Some motel owners complained about extra-musical activities such as marathon drinking, prostitution, brawling, and rooms rented to couples that might contain up to a dozen people, or more. On the other hand, restaurants doubled their customary volume of business over the Festival weekend, and alcohol sales skyrocketed. One liquor store near the fairgrounds claimed to gross nine thousand dollars over the weekend, three times normal volume, by staying open from six a.m. to two a.m. "These people don't go to bed," the manager noted.

George "Bob" Faul, former president of Monterey Peninsula College, was a member of the Festival Board of Directors throughout this period and recalls it as a time of social turmoil, "laced with lots and lots of marijuana," a time when you had to be ready for just about anything, including the defusing of potentially "volatile situations." The music itself often took a backseat to extracurricular activities. Faul remembers the area being "awash" with recreational vehicles, many of which offered carnal

delights that could never be advertised in the Festival program. Finally, Monterey's city fathers had to step in and apply some rules. Did they limit commerce to one or two RVs per block? No, they cut it off completely. Faul credits the Monterey Police Department with policing the area throughout an intractable time, playing it "pretty damn cool." Writing in 1962, esteemed critic Nat Hentoff deviated from the Festival's musical program long enough to praise Monterey Police Chief Charles Simpson, a man whose ability to play Scrabble in five languages impressed him. On the day the Hell's Angels arrived *en masse*, Simpson suddenly halted the stage show and the notorious motorcycle gang was just as suddenly swallowed up by a press of fans who, thinking it must be intermission time, headed for the bathrooms. In the mid-Sixties, the police force deliberately revamped its image. Officers wore "Smokey Bear" uniforms, the gentle khaki of caregivers not cops.

In the late Sixties, however, civil unrest grew so intense that security forces were imported from San Francisco. They came dressed for the occasion, and they were *not* benign nor inconspicuous. These were no Smokey Bear cops. Faul's wife, Pat, was seated with her nine-year-old daughter in the Main Arena. On a hot Saturday afternoon, prominent security personnel looked like "storm troopers from Nazi Germany," complete with helmets, leather boots, night sticks on ready alert. "Big Mama" Willie Mae Thornton was on stage when, suddenly, a young man in the middle of the arena stood up on his chair absolutely naked, waving his arms and having a grand old time in time to the music. As the troopers stormed the aisle, the crowd, who also had been joyously clapping, began to yell, "Go away, Pigs!" Ed Haber, a member of the Board of Directors readily identifiable by his red jacket, came down the aisle and spoke briefly to the police, and they left. Haber asked the young man to step down from his private dance pavilion, and escorted him safely from the arena. "Big Mama" resumed her song. "Amazing," Pat Faul says, "if the police had persisted, there would have been a gigantic riot."

Harry Crawford, who has served as usher coordinator since 1980, recalls the 1969 Festival appearance of Sly and the Family Stone. Lyons introduced the rock star by warning the audience about mounds of amps that had encumbered the stage, "There are twenty-millimeter cannons pointing at you and they're

all going to go off at the same time." Partially into his set, Stone refused to go on because a stool he customarily used had been misplaced, delaying the set for half an hour while the singer shouted obscenities at stage hands who were desperate to find the precious article. When they did, he began to play again and won the crowd over with his exhortations of "Hi-ya! Hi-ya!"

The times *were* a-changin'. It was not strictly rock music that invaded the Monterey Jazz Festival but its wild, untrammeled, unpredictable, impassioned spirit. Families of commune dwellers brought flutes and bongos and conga drums – a group "with *rhythm* coming out of them," according to Crawford. They mingled with people dressed to the nines: women in lavish gowns, men decked out in their Sunday best right down to brightly burnished new shoes. Everyone carted portable coolers or large wooden triptych bar units. Although he was not opposed to the good times, critic Philip Elwood believed that "Monterey jazz became more festival than music."

Harry Crawford recalls a Saturday afternoon when he took his grandmother to witness the spectacle. They sat in the middle of the arena and were having a fine time when someone turned around in his seat and handed her a joint. "You want some of this?" Grandma had no idea what he was offering, a fact that gradually dawned on her benefactor, who drawled, "Ah, you're having such a great time, you don't *need* any of this." Later, when Crawford's grandmother realized what had transpired – or not transpired – she was amused by the invitation, so typical of that all too generous age.

BELOW: A surprise spectator, Miles Davis, takes time off from his own 1969 musical chores to sit among the crowd enjoying the Buddy Guy Blues Band and Bobby Bryant and the Monterey Jazz Festival Soul All-Stars on a sunny Saturday afternoon. OPPOSITE: Simultaneous with the rock onslaught, Saturday afternoon also remained devoted to the blues, as provided by great singers such as Jimmy Rushing. Rushing is shown here with Benny Carter, left, and Ben Webster.

DIE-HARD FANS

It happens every year just after the Monterey Jazz Festival ends. Production coordinator David Murray picks up the phone and responds to a request for tickets for the next year's event. Hanging up, he shakes his head and grins. "They have no idea who's going to play. *We* have little idea. The event is a full year away and plans aren't even underway yet. Yet they still want to come. Why? Because it's the Monterey Jazz Festival, that's why."

By 1973, Festival fans were zealots. The days of overt musical experimentation were, for the most part, over. The Festival was no longer seeking an audience. It had one that was faithful to the core. Fans and musicians alike were part of a large extended family, and no one wanted to miss out on the reunion. Main Stage tickets became inheritance items. Or even items of contention in divorce suits. Writer/photographer Rick Carroll recalls, "My first wife got the box seats and I got the early Miles and Brubeck records." Second wife around, *she* got the silver Porsche, but he kept the front row seats. "I never regretted it," Carroll says. "Porsches, like wives, come and go, but Monterey remains."

Another couple continued to attend the Festival after they split up, but no longer able to sit beside each other, took new seats on opposite sides of the arena. Music heals, and distance can play strange tricks on the eyes of a beholder. After a few years, the couple remarried. But the final outcome has not always been so amicable. A woman wrote the Festival office saying she and her husband were getting a divorce. She could no longer stand the sight of him and asked if one of them could have a new seat, as far from their original seats as possible.

ABOVE: *Saxophonist Red Holloway, far left, and blues favorites B.B. King and Eddie "Cleanhead" Vinson, far right, are shown here with Etta James. Die-hard fan and midway concessioner Bill Welch ran a Louisiana catfish stand that the popular James plugged during a set on the Garden Stage. When business suddenly picked up as a result, Welch made an emergency run to a K-Mart in the city of Seaside for more supplies. On the way back he got held up in traffic. The Festival was being broadcast live and, as Welch tells it, "I see the people in their cars, I see the people sittin' at the bus stops, and I see the people walkin' down the street and man, everybody was rockin'. I said, 'What's goin' on here?' People was rockin' all the way down through Seaside and back into Monterey." Welch rolled down his window and recognized the sound. On the Festival's Main Stage, "Etta James was tearin' the place apart!"*
OPPOSITE: *Over the years, die-hard Festival fans acquired perennial favorite performers, such as the suave maestro Duke Ellington, shown here exhorting tenor saxophonist Paul Gonsalves to uncharted improvisational heights.*

ABOVE: Percy Heath, bassist with the Modern Jazz Quartet, not only enjoyed that group's frequent Festival appearances, but also performed with his brothers Jimmy and "Tootie" as part of a "Family Night" program Jimmy Lyons presented in 1973. BELOW: Die-hard fans loved the inimitable Count Basie, shown here (right) leading his orchestra, drummer Butch Miles to the left. Although a 1976 heart attack sidelined the great pianist/band leader, he was back at the Festival in 1977, as strong as ever. OPPOSITE: Husband-and-wife vocal team, Roy Kral and Jackie Cain appeared in 1973 when Jimmy Lyons closed out the final performance with "Family Night." The tone of the Festival shifted that Sunday evening. The days of overt experimentation were for the most part over. The Festival was no longer seeking an audience. It had one, faithful to the core. From 1973 to 1992, fans and musicians alike became kin. "Family Night" featured musicians from the Jones, Heath, Candoli, Turrentine, Rowles and Kral clans. The audience may have regarded the Festival as a family affair for some time, but that last night in 1973 canonized the notion by placing an official stamp on family ties and familiar faces.

Office coordinator Mary Piazza wrote back saying the couple would have to submit a request in writing (or have a lawyer do so). A letter from the wife arrived asking for a new seat for herself, relinquishing the old, granting it, magnanimously, to her ex-husband. Suspicious of the handwriting, Piazza phoned the woman. "What letter?" she responded. Her husband had not only submitted the request in her name, but forged her signature as well.

Tickets are not just coveted by parting husbands and wives. Piazza received a frantic phone call from a ticket holder in Florida during a hurricane. Due to the cacophony of wind, rain, and airborne debris thrashing about in the background, she had trouble understanding the man shouting that his car was running in the driveway. His house was about to be swept away, but all he could say was, "*Where* are my Festival tickets? I'm afraid the mailbox will get blown away after I leave. *Where* are my tickets?"

A surprising discovery is that, in spite of such zeal, many die-hard fans – although obviously fond of jazz music – admit they are not necessarily genuine jazz aficionados. "I wouldn't call myself a hard core jazz fan," Bill Lindsay, a biology instructor and box-seat holder for many years, admits. "I like jazz, but I don't know the names of everybody. I listen to the music and enjoy it, but I don't go to hear particular people."

Yet some die-hard fans have been fortunate enough to "hang" or hobnob with their favorite artists. Naomi Meyer is a front box holder. She ended up with eight prize seats smack in front of the stage after *her* divorce, plus access to the Hunt Club, a VIP bar adjacent to the Main Stage. There, Meyer met Paul Desmond whom she described as "very much a gentleman." She also recalls seeing Jimmy Witherspoon, but missed him the year after "he got a little outrageous," calling out to the audience during a performance, "How 'bout some coke for the Spoon?" He wasn't invited back again.

Photographer Will Wallace's Festival attendance predates his interest in shooting pictures. He started out as an usher in 1969. At that time the Festival was, in Wallace's words, "well known, and anybody that knew anything about jazz had always wanted to go to Mecca, so to speak." In those days, being an usher was also a very classy thing. The women wore white by day and black by night. Everyone wore formal red capes. Yet Wallace didn't remain an usher for long. Musicians were issued ID badges to admit them to the Hunt Club, but they could be careless about wearing them, or just refused to do so. One night blues singer Joe Williams was denied admission by a Rent-a-Cop. He returned with an irate Jimmy Lyons and, because Wallace was well informed on the jazz scene and knew all the musicians by sight, he was hired to screen incoming traffic. "I was thrilled," Wallace recalls. "I became a little lightweight cop, and it was fun." He admits he's not "running buddies" with the musicians, but he came to know several well: Dizzy Gillespie and Hank Jones (both avid photographers), Clark Terry, and Percy Heath. "If they wanted to talk about something, I just let it flow," he says. "I was there to listen, and they were there to say it."

Bill Welch first attended the Monterey

LEFT: Younger brother of Percy and Jimmy Heath, Albert "Tootie" Heath was regarded as a superb hard-bop drummer who had recorded with John Coltrane, J.J. Johnson and pianists Cedar Walton, Bobby Timmons and Herbie Hancock by the time he performed at "Family Night" in 1973. Heath is shown here in 1993 when he appeared with Orrin Keepnews' Riverside Reunion.

Jazz Festival in 1961, and later ran a Louisiana catfish concession on the midway. He not only talked with the musical artists – he also *fed* them. His favorite acquaintance was Etta James. While he was chatting with her just before a Garden Stage set, she said, "Baby, what's you doin?" He replied, "I got some Louisiana catfish down here." "Catfish!" she cried. "Yeah," Welch replied, "Cajun style." James said, "You know, I'm gonna tell these people about you." And she did. At break time the line in front of booth seventeen was *long*. Welch took Etta James a free catfish dinner, but the personal physician who traveled with her took one look at the rich lovely meal and said, "No catfish; definitely no catfish."

Not every ardent Festival fan has been fortunate enough to befriend artists, nor have one plug his or her concession stand, but that hasn't diminished their enthusiasm. Many die-hard fans feel the Festival has remarkable staying power, a constant with fine music and good times always in abundance. Others wax nostalgic for the "good old days," an attitude that does not prevent them from attending year after year. Bill Lindsay is one of the former. "The Festival has remained fairly consistent," he claims, chock full of memories of fans such as the group, seated across from his box, who set out a classy tablecloth on the wall in front of them, adorning it with silver goblets, champagne in an elegant bucket, and candelabra each year, along with ornate silverware for their hors d'oeuvres. A tad more pedestrian perhaps, Lindsay's own group retaliated with a sheet which they draped from their box, asking people to sign it. "It became

a giant greeting card," Bill Lindsay says now, "with probably one-hundred-fifty signatures or more." One year the group auctioned off a trophy given to a former employee-of-the-month at Jack-in-the-Box.

Carmel resident Hans Lehmann, a regular since 1972, calls the Monterey Jazz Festival "the high point of my social year." He started out with a nucleus of twelve ticket holders, many from the San Francisco Bay Area. The Saturday afternoon blues fete would spill over into a pot luck party at his house. "We would pass out small maps," he says, "and invite all kinds of people, and everybody came!" Lehmann observes that, now, a certain warmth, an ethnicity that once characterized the event, is gone. "It's no reflection on the music," Lehmann says, "the music hasn't changed to that extent. But there used to be more spontaneity, even frivolity, that isn't there anymore." He never had a problem dancing on Saturday, he claims. "In the old days, all of a sudden, when they hit that *one note*, the whole audience was on their chairs." Recent Saturdays have been more subdued, self-conscious. "Even the aisles are slimmer," he says, suspecting a fire marshal's conspiracy to tone down the event. Lehmann admits he may just be getting older. Many of the artists he grew up on and loved are gone. Dizzy. Louis. Earl "Fatha" Hines. Woody. Sarah. "If the musicians are dying," he says, "the audience is dying too." He misses what he calls "the camaraderie, the sense of being one family."

But, Lehmann adds, "It's still the highlight of my year."

BELOW: Die-hard fans couldn't get enough of Duke Ellington or Woody Herman, and in 1970 they got the two for the price of one. Ellington, left, and Herman, second from left, are shown here with members of the former's orchestra, left to right, Paul Gonsalves on tenor saxophone, Joe Benjamin on bass and Harold Ashby, tenor saxophone. OPPOSITE: Fans have lists of favorite performances and performers and high on those lists are Sarah Vaughan and Billy Eckstine who are shown here in a 1981 performance.

FAMILIAR FACES

Let critics carp. "They're paid to criticize," Jimmy Lyons said, "that's what they do." Ralph J. Gleason, Lyon's friend to the end, despite all his harsh criticism, died in 1975. Many of the various tributaries that had nourished the Festival in its early mom-and-pop store days had fallen away or dwindled, giving general manager Lyons free reign. He enjoyed and took advantage of it, genuinely sincere – in the view of critic Philip Elwood – about the Festival's legitimacy in preserving mainstream jazz. Lyons knew what he liked. Die-hard Festival fans knew what they liked. And fortunately, for the event's financial destiny, these new partners agreed. If Festival fans couldn't get enough of Woody Herman or Sarah Vaughan, well then, Lyons would give them Woody and Sarah. The event acquired a set format filled with familiar faces, but the format worked.

There were many things the Festival *might* have done or *could* have done, but, given budgetary constraints, Lyons did very well. If Lyons' taste ran to bebop, big bands and mainstream music, well, so be it. Guitarist Mundell Lowe was a member of the Festival house band for fifteen years, and musical director for four years. "If he had the dollar to work with, and of course in those days we didn't have what you have now," Lowe says, "Jimmy was a very fair-minded man." As for criticism, Mississippi-born Lowe believes that, trying to hold a big vehicle like the Festival in the middle of the road, the person in the driver's seat has got to listen to "all this claptrap or whatever it is, and then make his own decisions." Which he believes Lyons did – "straight ahead."

By the fourth decade, thirteen artists had

ABOVE: In 1977, Woody Herman, right, teamed up with ex-sideman Stan Getz for a memorable performance on "What Are You Doing the Rest of Your Life?" After a 1979 performance by the Herman Band, critic Leonard Feather described the clarinetist/leader as "the grand survivor of the big band epoch," a man who learned to adjust to changing circumstances so well that "he and his young sidemen are prepared to do anything short of turning handsprings." OPPOSITE: In 1987, Clark Terry upstaged the Pope in Monterey. John Paul II was about to arrive in the city to offer silent prayer at the grave site of Father Junipero Serra, founder of the California missions. Yet the Pope only managed a small insert photo on the cover of Monterey Life magazine, which read, "Monterey Jazz Turns 30" and featured a huge photo of Terry. Not bad for a man whose first childhood trumpet was a section of coiled-up, discarded garden hose tied with wire to shape valves, a kerosene funnel stuck on one end for a bell and a piece of lead pipe on the other for a mouthpiece.

RIGHT: Oscar Peterson first appeared at the Festival in 1959. His trio included Ray Brown on bass and Ed Thigpen on drums. The popular pianist returned to delight audiences in 1968, 1971 and 1990. OPPOSITE: In 1976, a "Basie Retrospective" featured the extraordinary former Basie drummer Jo Jones – or, as introduced by Jimmy Lyons, "Someone who dropped in out of the sky, unbeknownst to anyone." The retrospective featured the Kansas City Seven, with Jones on drums; Nat Pierce on piano, who replicated Basie's notes if not his touch; ever faithful guitarist Freddie Green's steady plunk strum; "Sweets" Edison, Vic Dickenson, Buddy Tate, and John Heard. On a swinging good time blues, the unbeknownst Jones was cool, sprightly and brightly conspicuous, as only he could be.

appeared a total of one hundred thirty-nine times at the Monterey Jazz Festival. That's not counting Dizzy Gillespie – who could pop up at any time, invited or not – or John Lewis, who had been musical director for more than twenty years. Aside from Gillespie and Lewis, the Festival's most "frequent flier" is Clark Terry, an all-purpose player whom fans adore. Terry has appeared nineteen times. The Modern Jazz Quartet has seventeen official engagements. Mundell Lowe has sixteen and, according to the official programs, blues singer Joe Williams made fourteen appearances, Cal Tjader ten, Dave Brubeck ten, Woody Herman nine; bassist Ray Brown, Carmen McRae and Jon Hendricks tied at eight; Sarah Vaughan, Duke Ellington and percussionist Poncho Sanchez all made seven.

CLARK TERRY

Informed of his top number of appearances, Clark Terry responds, modestly, "If it's the record, I shall cherish it." As a participating musician, Terry had no hangups at all, no ego problems. He would play with anybody. Asked to back up someone, he did. Asked to work with the California High School All-Star Big Band, he did. Terry's versatility was born out again and again, and his performances were superb, far more than just the labors of an accomplished utility man. When the flugelhorn player did duets with bassist Red Mitchell in 1987, and someone yelled "Play blues!", Terry invented lyrics on the spot, words both funny and wise. At the 1974 Festival, Terry was a guest artist with the Dizzy Gillespie Quartet.

BELOW: Thad Jones conducts one of many fine big bands to appear at the Festival: the Thad Jones-Mel Lewis Orchestra. The bassist is Ray Drummond. OPPOSITE: Milt Jackson, vibraphonist with the perennial favorite, the Modern Jazz Quartet. Writing about a "Porgy and Bess Medley" presented at the 1964 Festival, critic Don DeMicheal commented that Jackson "gave 'My Man's Gone' such blue hell that bassist Percy Heath, usually the picture of dignity on stage, turned his head from his written part and stared, smiling as if awestruck, at Jackson flailing his vibraharp."

That Sunday afternoon, he performed as soloist with the California High School All-Star Big Band; and that night, after participating in a "Latin Jam – Inventions on Manteca" with Cal Tjader, Mongo Santamaria, and Airto Moreira, he joined Japan's Toshiyuki Miyama and the New Herd to close out that year's Festival. The secret of such flexibility? "Just to be happy to be involved with something you love doing for a livelihood," he explains. It's difficult to take Terry seriously when he says that he always dreamed of such opportunities but never really thought they'd come to him.

Besides specific musical performances, what Terry remembers most about Monterey is the "beautiful camaraderie of seeing all those people backstage" at the Festival. The Hunt Club bar was available, but musicians pre-ferred to congregate on a small crowded stairway. "You'd see people you hadn't seen in ages," Terry says. He recalls the last time he had a chance to hang out with Billy Eckstine. Terry also got a big kick out of seeing Darlene Chan looking through the peephole stage manager Paul Vieregge had installed for her. "It was about two feet off the ground," Clark Terry claims. Others remember Terry as well. After Mundell Lowe was married at Doc Rickett's lab on Cannery Row, tender sounds filled the misty night. Terry was playing "When I Fall in Love" from the balcony.

MODERN JAZZ QUARTET

John Lewis on piano, Milt Jackson vibes, Percy Heath bass, and Connie Kay drums made seventeen official appearances at the Monterey Jazz Festival. Under the stewardship of Lewis, the popular group became known for its dignity and refinement, a nearly *classical* chamber jazz approach to the music, mixed with deep bop roots, Milt Jackson's passion for the blues, and the ability, within and beyond it all, to swing. The Modern Jazz Quartet enjoyed a long – thirty-seven year – tenure together, reuniting even after they'd once broken up. Percy Heath says people have asked him how he could hang in there with one group that long and not get bored. He replies, "Because it was *never* the same." No single performance was the same as another. People didn't realize the extent of genuine improvisation taking place.

Heath, whom Lyons always introduced as "the world's greatest fisherman who plays bass," has bright memories of the Festival as well. On Thursday night staff and musicians have always come together for a pre-Festival barbecue. One year, Heath caught a twenty-one pound, forty-seven inch Atlantic bluefish the day before he was to leave for Monterey. He packed the fish, along with smaller specimens, in dry ice and had it sent on ahead to the West Coast, along with his bass. Festival chef Leon Smith assumed Heath would do the cooking, but when they unpacked the fish it was still frozen. Heath put it on the grill and cooked it slowly, turning the fish over, cooking the fish a layer at a time, scraping it off, turning it over, going back to repeat the process again and again. Finished, this gourmet delight "looked like one of those cartoon fish," Heath says today, "with just the *head* and *bones*."

Like other musicians, Heath considered the Monterey Jazz Festival "quite a presti-

RIGHT: Photojournalist Peter Breinig had the good fortune to know the stunning vocalist Carmen McRae (shown here) fairly well. "She was a stickler for making lyrics meaningful," Breinig says. "If she sang a lyric, she figured out what it was saying and then tried to provide the right emphasis and phrasing. A lot of singers don't do this; they sing a particularly poignant turn of the lyrics with the same emphasis they put on everything else. But Carmen wanted those lyrics to mean something."

gious affair; everybody made it." Just as Lyons would tell Clark Terry, "Put it in your book for next year," as soon as the Festival was over, the Modern Jazz Quartet's manager made sure the group wasn't booked for other fall gigs until after the September event. The Festival was the kickoff for their autumn season: after Percy Heath returned from summer fishing with his sons of course, and just before the group would take off for Europe or Japan for three to four weeks on the road.

Lyons had a definite preference for big band jazz, and a host of such aggregates graced the Main Stage throughout the Festival's history. Duke Ellington's orchestra, of course, from the start. And Count Basie's. One of Basie's vocalists, blues singer Joe Williams has made at least fourteen appearances at Monterey, with or without the great Basie band. That group itself appeared five times, starting in 1959 and was still going strong in 1976, when its leader was sidelined by a heart attack. Count Basie was back at the Festival with the band in 1977, in writer Ira Kamin's words, "healthy, sparse and beaming."

Other big bands that appeared at Monterey were those of Harry James, Terry Gibbs, Quincy Jones, Don Ellis, Buddy Rich, Louie Bellson, Stan Kenton, Thad Jones and Mel Lewis, Toshiko Akiyoshi, Ed Shaughnessy, Maynard Ferguson, and Toshiyuki Miyama. The Airmen of Note appeared, along with Gerald Wilson's Band of the '80s, Rob McConnell's Boss Brass Big Band, Bill Berry and the L.A. Big Band, Lionel Hampton and His Orchestra, Ann Patterson's Maiden Voyage, the Capp-Pierce Juggernaut, Bob Florence's Limited Edition, plus groups led by Bill Holman and Illinois Jacquet. It's an impressive list. Yet for all the rich, roaring, sometimes stertorous music these aggregates provided, the band – or bands, since he went through a succession of "herds" – that stands out most in many fans' minds, and hearts, is Woody Herman's.

WOODY HERMAN

The clarinetist made nine appearances at the Monterey Jazz Festival between his first spectacular well-rehearsed showing in 1959 – when saxophone stalwarts Zoot Sims, Richie Kamuca and Bill Perkins played behind Coleman Hawkins, Ben Webster and Ornette Coleman – and his final Thundering Herd appearance in 1985, two years before he died.

Herman's bands presented classic arrangements of tunes such as "Apple Honey," "Caldonia," "Northwest Passage," "Four Brothers" "The Goof and I," "Early Autumn," a 1967 world premiere of Bill Holman's "Concerto for Herd," adaptions by pianist Alan Broadbent of "Blues in the Night," and Frank Tiberi of John Coltrane's "Countdown."

Whenever the popular bandleader came to the West Coast, both Gleason and Lyons would sit up until four in the morning with him, talking about who was now playing with whom, and what was *really* happening in the music business. A member of the Festival Board of Directors for twenty years, Sam Karas and his wife Edie once took Woody Herman and his wife out for dinner. In awe, Karas said, "Geez, my wife and I danced to you on our honeymoon." Herman's response was, "*Every* couple in America danced on their honeymoon to our band."

PAUL DESMOND

Pianist Dave Brubeck appeared ten times at Monterey, with his famous quartet featuring Paul Desmond on alto sax and, after that group split up in 1967, with either Gerry Mulligan, clarinetist Bill Smith, or his son Chris on electric bass and bass trombone. Paul Desmond was as popular a Festival figure as Brubeck. Later, on his own and eight months before he died of cancer, Desmond brought a quartet that included Canadian guitarist Ed Bickert to Monterey. On this occasion, Desmond played "A Day in the Life of a Fool." The immaculate phrasing, the impeccable tone, the fine structure of his solos, the tasty pauses and sustained mood (even a witty seamless quote from "Stardust") were all still there.

Even as his death approached, Desmond never lost his sense of humor. He told friends that he kept having a nightmare that, placed on an operating table, he would look up and see author George Plimpton – who specialized in writing books about amateur adventures as a stand-in quarterback or symphony conductor – standing over him, ready (or not so ready) for surgery. Desmond loved Lyons' Big Sur log cabin located on a ridge overlooking a canyon, and he asked that his ashes be scattered in the latter. Lyons took the ashes and a shaker full of martinis, which Desmond also loved, up in a plane piloted by photographer Peter Breinig. "We dropped swiftly down into the canyon," Breinig recalls, "and Jimmy scattered the ashes outside the right side window." The second pass was less successful. Lyons

ABOVE: Among the host of exceptional female vocalists to appear at the Festival, Betty Carter has been one of the most original, dynamic and consistently rewarding performers. She first appeared in 1975, and returned in 1977 and 1992.

finished *his own* martini but when he attempted to throw one out the window for Desmond, the liquid flew back in his face.

Just as the Festival parade of frequent visits by big bands and fine instrumentalists such as Brubeck and Desmond is impressive, so is its historical array of vocalists from the early performances (1958-1965) by Lizzie Miles, Velma Middleton (with Louis Armstrong), Jimmy Witherspoon, Joe Williams, Helen Humes, Odetta; Lambert, Hendricks and Ross; Lambert, Hendricks and Bavan; Helen Merrill, Marlena Shaw, Mary Stallings, Anita O'Day, to a middle period (1966-1972) featuring Carol Sloane, Mel Torme, Billy Eckstine, Al Hibbler, Roberta Flack, and Dee Dee Bridgewater, to a later period (1973 to 1991) that offered Betty Carter, Ruth Brown, the Hi-Lows, Manhattan Transfer, Diane Schuur, Bobby McFerrin, Tania Maria, Flora Purim, Ernestine Anderson, Linda Hopkins and Dianne Reeves. In the midst of all this vocal wealth, two names stand out, two singers who returned again and again, two singers whom crowds couldn't get enough of. Ironically, those same fans would eventually – through their inadvertent enthusiasm or rudeness – drive one of the two away, for good.

SARAH VAUGHAN

The singer who stayed was the irrepressible Sarah, much loved for the magic she could work even on show tunes such as "Send in the Clowns." The Festival's education program coordinator, Stella LePine started out as a Festival driver and was assigned to pick up Vaughan at the Hyatt Hotel. "We had brand new Oldsmobiles in those days," LePine recalls, "and to me that was a big deal." Arriving, she rang Vaughan's room. "Where will the limo be?" was the response. "Limo? It's only an Oldsmobile," LePine replied. "Well," Vaughan said, "*we* do not ride in Oldsmobiles." And she wouldn't. LePine returned to the Festival office and had to locate a limousine to escort "Sassy" to that evening's concert. The very human Vaughan was divine when she started to sing. Following a 1978 Festival appearance, *Billboard's* Eliot Tiegel called her "the premier female jazz singer" of the day.

CARMEN MCRAE

McRae appeared at the Monterey Jazz Festival on eight occasions, and each time she worked more than a little magic of her own. In 1961, Ralph Gleason had written about her

"visual and vocal beauty," after she hushed an audience of 7,300 with her version of "When Sunny Gets Blue." Introduced by Lyons in 1971 as "my favorite lady of song, the Queen; please welcome with all the love you have," McRae sang a slow ballad, "I Wish I Knew." With fine backing by guitarist Joe Pass, she gently provoked those involuntary goose bumps Vaughan was famous for. The vocalist's phrasing, pauses, emphasis, accents – "Did I mistake this . . . *for* . . . a real romance?" – are perfect. "I'm a fool" comes across as bitter, harsh, but the last phrase, "I wish I *knew*" is heartbreaking: tender, fully human, obsequious but plaintive.

The vocalist appeared at a special Thursday night performance to celebrate the Festival's twenty-fifth, or silver anniversary in 1982. The audience, which included members of the Festival staff and ushers who'd been partying all afternoon, was so loud and rude that McRae lambasted them from the microphone. She vowed never to come back again and Carmen McRae kept her pledge. She never returned to the Monterey Jazz Festival.

McRae's Festival demise was by choice, but another factor began to affect the presence or absence of familiar faces at Monterey as the years went by. Some *couldn't* show up, for the ultimate reason. Duke Ellington passed away in 1974. Paul Desmond in 1977, Cal Tjader in 1982. Woody Herman died in 1987, Sarah Vaughan in 1990. Carmen McRae herself would make her final departure in 1994.

BELOW: Ironically, in the days before the great Dave Brubeck Quartet featuring Paul Desmond on alto saxophone was formed, the latter walked off with members of a group Brubeck worked with, and hired another pianist for a club date on the Feather River. As a result of this betrayal, Brubeck said he never wanted to speak to or see Desmond again in his life. Fortunately, the pianist's wife, who liked Desmond and thought he and her husband sounded great together, patched things up. The result was the quartet that thrilled so many fans in the Festival's early days. OPPOSITE: The incomparable Sarah Vaughan offers her signature song, "Send in the Clowns."

MORE BLUES,
THE LATIN TINGE and THE JAPAN CONNECTION

The Saturday afternoon blues show – inaugurated in 1964 with Jon Hendricks' "The Blues – Right Now!" – had become a Festival mainstay by 1973. While the program remained loose and lively, it was also locked into place, no longer a request on the part of its audience, but a demand. For some fans, the Saturday afternoon blues show constituted the *real* Monterey Jazz Festival, the one event they were certain to attend. Yet, while this show and a steady diet of familiar faces continued to draw capacity crowds, the Festival also branched out into other areas. Latin jazz became increasingly popular and many Latin artists were added to the event's menu. "Sleepy" Matsumoto's 1963 appearance marked the start of Festival ties with Japan that would grow stronger, until those ties were fixed permanently and Japanese artists appeared each year.

MORE BLUES

The Saturday afternoon blues show kept its carnival atmosphere. Fans who couldn't sit still for the regular shows – dancers with anxious nimble feet, people who preferred music they could *move* to – flocked to the Saturday afternoon fête. From 1973 on, blues fans got their fill of top names: Jimmy Rogers and his Chicago Blues Band, Mance Lipscomb, the Reverend Pearly Brown, Sunnyland Slim, James Cotton, Bobby "Blue" Bland, Son Seals, John Hammond, Willie Dixon, Percy Mayfield, Lowell Fulson, Robert Cray, Johnny Otis, Linda Hopkins, Carla Thomas, Katie Webster, Little Milton, Jimmy McCracklin, Charlie Musslewhite, Floyd Dixon – the list goes on and on.

ABOVE: In 1977, New Orleans invaded the Main Stage for the first time when Jimmy Lyons offered "Mardis Gras at Monterey." The great guitarist/violinist Clarence "Gatemouth" Brown was featured along with the delightful vocalist Queen Ida, with her shoulder-shrugging "C'est La Vie." OPPOSITE: By the 1958 Festival, Cal Tjader, who was once Dave Brubeck's drummer, had switched to vibraphone full time, and Latin music as well. After Tjader started his own group, writer Ron Wynn called him "the greatest non-Latin band leader in Latin jazz history."

TOP: Known as the "Swamp Boogie Queen," the vibrant Katie Webster – with a repertoire of more than three thousand songs, ranging from New Orleans R & B to gospel to boogie woogie – was a popular Saturday afternoon blues show performer who made Festival appearances in 1988, 1990 and 1992. ABOVE: Musician, singer, lawyer and actor Ruben Blades, a genuine Renaissance man of the Nineties, would cap the Festival influx of Latin music in 1993 with an impassioned performance that lasted until 1:45 in the morning. The four-time Grammy nominee, who successfully mixes politics with music ("Playing with my band is like dancing with the truth," Blades says, "and she likes it"), also announced he would be running for president of Panama in 1994. OPPOSITE: In 1987, Eddie "Cleanhead" Vinson left his personal stamp just about everywhere at the Festival. A hit on the Main Stage, Vinson was an even bigger hit later on the Garden Stage.

Mark Naftalin, who had appeared with the Paul Butterfield Blues Band in 1966, assembled his first Rhythm and Blues Review in 1981, a task with joyful results he would repeat on either the Main Stage or Garden Stage through 1992, presenting many blues greats. The years before Naftalin was in charge were filled with alternative blues shows such as 1979's "Mardi Gras Mambo – the Sounds of New Orleans," which featured the Neville Brothers Band, Dr. John, and the Wild Tchoupitoulas, who were dressed in outrageous beaded and plumed costumes. The spectacle drew brief comment from esteemed critic Leonard Feather. He wrote that the once memorable celebration of the blues had "degenerated drastically" and that he hoped Lyons would set the Festival back on the right track by restoring "the pristine blues beauty of his original Saturday matinee concept." On the other hand, critic Joel Selvin wrote that the Mardi Gras fête was "what a major festival like the Monterey Jazz Festival should be all about": infectious rhythms, singing, dancing, pageantry, presenting a "distinctive and flavorful indigenous regional style of R&B."

Buddy Guy (with gospel-ordained strident shouts, nearly out of control, hoarse cries of anguish: "Should have heard me beggin', blues don't murder me!") and Junior Wells (with a more reflective submerged pain and bitter laughter; then full vocal range from cellar to sky: "Anybody, anybody . . . anybody seen my baby, *please* send her back to me!") were always great favorites. And in 1987 Ray Charles turned up on Friday night, with his hair turned gray, to plunge the Festival crowd into youthful frenzy with "What'd I Say?" The next year, Albert Collins tore the Main Stage apart with screaming guitar licks, then wandered out to pay his respects among the crowd. A strong 1991 blues show featured three jazz-oriented performers: Floyd Dixon, Charles Brown and Ruth Brown, the first two veterans still in top form. Saturday afternoon was alive and well, and would continue to be for years to come.

THE LATIN TINGE

Pianist/composer Jelly Roll Morton coined the term "Spanish Tinge" for the *habanera*, or tango, rhythms he occasionally employed in his left hand, rhythms he claimed were essential to jazz. The term "Latin" gets applied to a wide range of jazz-oriented music today, and a host of disparate geographical sources from the Caribbean and Cuba to Brazil,

Argentina, New York (with its more aggressive stance) and Los Angeles (with its more laid-back West Coast musical posture). "Latin" has come to mean both samba and salsa, but the instrumental ingredients – conga drums, bongos, cowbells, *shekeres* (a gourd strung with beads), *timbales* – and above all the infectious danceable rhythm, the thick percussive textures – have grown quite familiar, and favorable, to Festival regulars. In 1947, when Dizzy Gillespie paired off with Cuban percussionist Chano Pozo, they gave birth to Afro-Cuban jazz, or "cubop," and paved the way for the appreciation of this music. In 1958, Cal Tjader closed out the first Festival's second night with a Latin jam featuring percussionists Mongo Santamaria and Willie Bobo. Tjader returned in 1965 with conga drummer Armando Perazza, the leader providing fine unbroken lines, both lively and lovely, on "Violets for Your Furs," a piece full of subtle rhythmic effects. He then turned around and provided a fetching up tempo bossa nova groove on Antonio Carlos Jobim's "*Favela*." When an intruder barged on stage, Perazza jumped up, moving in time to Tjader's music, and danced the man right off the stage.

The 1960s bossa nova craze, fostered by Stan Getz (who made a Festival appearance with guitarist Jimmy Raney in 1962) and Astrud Gilberto, paved the way for the 1966 performance of Brazil's Bola Sete. Sete offered blazing guitar work on selections from the film *Black Orpheus* (1958): Luiz Bonfa's "*Manha De Carnaval*" and Jobim's "*A Felicidade*." But it wasn't until 1974 that the Latin fever truly took hold. On Sunday night, Lyons first presented one of the most sought-after percussionists in jazz, Airto Moriera; then "Latin Jam – Inventions on Manteca" which featured Gillespie, Tjader, Santamaria and Jerome Richardson with the Toshiyuki Miyama band. The appeal of this music entrenched (even in a band from Japan), the Festival would feature the popular Cal Tjader a total of ten times before his sudden death of a heart attack in the Philippines in 1982. His protégé Poncho Sanchez has continued Tjader's legacy, and has appeared at the Festival seven times himself. Another popular Latin Jazz figure, Tito Puente, first performed in 1977, when seven thousand people ended up dancing to his music in the rain. Puente's appeal was such that he returned five more times. In a 1982 interview, he said, "I was always looking forward to the beautiful mar-

LEFT: Guitarist Mundell Lowe, musical director from 1983 through 1986 and member of a stellar "house" band for fifteen years, performs with Japanese clarinetist Eiji Kitamura, right, a Festival mainstay since his first appearance in 1977. Kitamura has been dubbed "the Benny Goodman of Japan," but he recalls Goodman's great pianist Teddy Wilson, with whom he performed in Japan in 1969, advising him to "keep your own idea," to develop his own unique approach and style, which he has – a style characterized by clarity, purity and a rich lovely wood tone.

riage of Latin music and jazz music getting together, and we're finally getting there."

THE JAPANESE CONNECTION

The first musical artist from Japan to appear at the Festival was Hidehiko "Sleepy" Matsumoto in 1963. Ralph Gleason regarded him as something of a novelty, saying he was "interesting only as a curiosity," but a future Board of Directors president, Joe Green who was attending his first Festival that year, recalls being impressed by Matsumoto's performance on a baritone sax "almost as big as he was." In 1974, the first of the big bands arrived from across the Pacific: the much respected Toshiyuki Miyama and the New Herd. A young pianist named "Go" Yamamoto walked on stage in 1977 during the twentieth anniversary "Blow Out," a giant jam session that included Clark Terry, "Sweets" Edison, "Lockjaw" Davis, Benny Golson, John Lewis, Cal Tjader and Richard Davis. Undaunted by such awesome company, and introduced by Lewis as "another very fine young guest from Japan," Yamamoto proceeded to steal the show with "Midnight Sun." His touch was superb, and his style, though based on that of Erroll Garner, contained a quirky originality that combined the Japanese aesthetic virtues of *yugen* (implying strong emotion without explicitly stating it) and *sabi* (austere simplicity tinged with melancholy). The piece built to a resounding close and someone called out "Ya-ma-mo-to!" even before the prolonged applause began.

On the same bill, clarinetist Eiji Kitamura appeared for his first time at Monterey. He has since become a perennial Festival figure and has escorted a number of fine Japanese musicians on each trip, including pianist Kotaro Tsukahara and guitarist Yoshiaki "Miya" Miyanoue. Tsukahara switched from classical music to jazz when he realized that people don't applaud between movements of a symphony. "They just cleared their throats," he says. In Japan, Miyanoue leads his own group called Smokin'. He is a dynamic artist who, à la Wes Montgomery, has developed a warm thumb pick/pluck/strum style, having practiced this method "up and down, up and down," for ten years. And Miyanoue adds, "most people cannot wait ten years for anything."

Since 1980, when the Tokyo Union Orchestra performed at Monterey, a Japanese big band has appeared nearly every year. In 1986, the Keio Light Music Society Big Band was considered the best collegiate jazz aggregate in Japan. Many of the groups that come to Monterey are amateur bands made up of excellent players whose day jobs range from engineer to school teacher to civil service employee. The Big Band of Rogues – a group whose "first love is music, but whose first job is not," according to an official program – is typical, along with the Swing Twilight Jazz Orchestra, the Swing Ace Band, and Osaka's Global Jazz Orchestra.

Toshiko Akiyoshi, who left Japan in 1956 to attend Berklee College of Music, has made five appearances in Monterey. A brilliant pianist, composer and arranger, her big band's most memorable Festival piece, called "*Kogun,*" made strong use of traditional Japanese musical elements. When Akiyoshi first started playing jazz, she felt the art form possessed *bata no nioi,* "the smell of butter" (the odor of strange or alien food fare), in the minds of her countrymen, but she decided to take a good look at her native heritage as a positive element. *"Kogun"* was written after she heard news of a Japanese soldier still hiding in the Philippines thirty years after the end of World War II. The title means "forlorn forces" or "alone." Akiyoshi uses the analogy of a pearl for incorporating traditional Japanese instruments in jazz. One integrates the irritation of a different sound (in this case, *tsuzumi* drums), but the goal is a blend or what she calls "one music." The results worked handsomely at Monterey.

SUNDAY'S ALL-STARS

"Music is something that chooses *you.* A lot of kids are touched by it. Some are going to have the great experience of having played music at a crucial time in their lives. Some – a very small percentage – may actually become professional musicians. Others may just remember it the way people remember their college days, as a fond period. The key to success is giving them victories. You don't make a kid memorize the dictionary. You let him speak a sentence. Then you show him another way to make that sentence better. Then you tickle him with still another way to say the same thing. These are the little victories, but you let the kids bring them out of themselves. You set them up to make the change. All you've got to do then is stay out of the way."

– Bruce Forman; *guitarist and educational program clinician*

Like so much of the Festival's history, its flourishing jazz education program had a tentative beginning, experienced some major growing pains, and – now serving 863 students in Monterey County alone – is regarded as a model for the rest of the nation. The program didn't fully click into place until it acquired the services of professional musicians such as Bruce Forman, a master guitarist who, although "uncredentialed" in the traditional sense, has come up with hands-on methods and solid results that are the envy of professional educators.

The process that led to hiring jazz artists as clinicians began, as other Festival ideas, with a "vision." In 1970 Jimmy Lyons featured the Oakland Youth Chamber Orchestra per-

ABOVE: Bill Berry has served as director of the California High School All-Star Big Band since 1981, the longest running tenure of anyone in that position. "I treat the kids just exactly like I treat my own band, exactly," he says. He does not play down to them. If they're going to be in the All-Star Band, they're going to play well or they won't stay. The kids react positively to this approach because this is the first time they've been in a situation where everyone else is as good as they are. They are the very best from each school and, as Berry says, "I've got them all together." OPPOSITE: An early favorite among Festival clinicians was easygoing, straight-ahead, no-nonsense guitar virtuoso Bruce Forman. He arrived for clinic sessions in faded jeans with a hole in the back pocket. He joked with the kids and they could relate to him. When he played, he played like a demon, and they wanted to be able to do that also. "Yeah, I'm on their level," Bruce Forman says now, laughing. "That must have been a bad pair of jeans." Bill Berry adds, "It's the same pair he's been wearing for years."

forming with such seasoned professionals as Bill Evans, the Modern Jazz Quartet, and Cannonball Adderley. In 1971, he formalized the commitment to youth by presenting, at the Festival's Sunday afternoon show, the winner of the first California High School Jazz Band Competition: the Ygnacio Valley High School Jazz Band. He also introduced members of the first California High School All-Star Big Band. If Lyons is likely to be remembered for any one thing, the event he initiated – then called "Jazz Today and Tomorrow" – may be it. It offered unprecedented musical opportunities for young musicians to learn their art.

Forman says, "Jimmy had a vision for this. What's happening has blossomed into something *great*, and everybody who's been involved deserves credit. But without Jimmy's vision in the beginning . . . to bring professional players into the mix with a student band, well, *that* was unique."

The Monterey Jazz Festival was founded as a non-profit educational organization. Advance publicity in 1958 stated that all profits would go toward establishing a chair of jazz at Monterey Peninsula College. While only two three-hundred-dollar scholarships were granted that first year, and 1959 losses precluded any scholarship funds, by 1970, thirty-five

thousand dollars had been granted to the college. Festival-supported musical activities included grants to the Carmel Bach Festival and the Monterey County Symphony. The Festival even came up with two-thousand dollars to import artists such as Cal Tjader and "Big Mama" Willie Mae Thornton to Soledad Correctional Facility for concerts. By 1970, a grand total of $77,977 had been distributed to various causes.

In the early days, however, accountability was a problem. Jokes still circulate about scholarship funds going for tap dancing classes, a drum and bugle corps or even choir robes at Monterey Peninsula College. Some measure of misunderstanding did exist between town and gown: the "town" in this case being the Festival Board of Directors. Its strictly jazz-oriented members were unhappy with the results of the educational funding program. Hoping to form closer ties with the community, to work from "the inside out," Monterey Peninsula College president Bob Faul became a member of the Board himself. He also hired pianist/arranger/educator Don Schamber in 1971, in hopes of establishing a better working relationship.

When Lyons inaugurated his "Jazz Today and Tomorrow" program in 1971, the timing seemed good – at least for a while. College

ABOVE: In 1971, Oliver Nelson, famous for his classic 1961 **Blues and the Abstract Truth** *recording, presented his "Berlin Dialogue for Orchestra." Later, he said he found the live Monterey version "better" than a recording he'd made of that piece. BELOW: Among the significant gene pools represented in the Festival's High School All-Star Big Band program was the Grenadier family, which produced Steve, on guitar, Phil, on trumpet, and Larry, on bass. The latter was featured in the 1996 recreation of Lalo Schifrin's "Gillespiana." Steve and Larry are shown here, performing together. The program also produced Chad Wackerman – who's worked with the Bill Watrous Big Band and Frank Zappa – and his brothers Bob and John who've played with Maynard Ferguson. OPPOSITE: In 1985, Dave Ellis played tenor saxophone with the High School All-Star Big Band. He returned to the Festival in 1994 as a member of the Charlie Hunter Trio, performed with Hunter's group on the Main Stage in 1995, and led his own trio in Dizzy's Den in 1996, also appearing with Mingus Amungus on the Garden Stage.*

ABOVE: *Ladd McIntosh was an All-Star Band musical director in the early Seventies. He was a talented composer and solid reed player who had established a jazz program at Westminster College in Utah, a man who sported Haight-Ashbury tie-dye trappings, complete with a wild mane of dark hair and a beard that descended to his belt buckle. One of his original pieces was entitled "Ooh, Mother Magnet, or Lord Buckley Rides Again." OPPOSITE: One of the most illustrious graduates of the Festival's High School All-Star Big Band program is tenor saxophonist Joshua Redman.*

facilities were used for auditions for the first California High School All-Star Big Band. A panel of judges listened to various groups competing for the high-school prize, then selected twenty All-Star players (five on trumpet, five on trombone, five on sax, plus a rhythm section of piano, bass, drums, guitar, and vibes) on the basis of individual merit. "The disaster of that," according to Schamber, is that, brought to the Festival fairgrounds to perform new work in September, the All-Star kids who had been selected "couldn't read." They had been performing specific charts with their respective schools all year, and knew *that* music inside and out. Yet they were stumped by the fresh charts placed before them. After this mishap, "kids were auditioned for their reading skills," Schamber says.

Throughout the Seventies, these young musicians were required to perform original compositions by Oliver Nelson, Ladd McIntosh, Mundell Lowe, Benny Golson, Don Ellis, Chuck Mangione, George Duke and David Friesen. The Sunday afternoon tradition of new original music was being maintained, but now such pieces were being performed by "the kids." Over the years, these performances allowed the students to rub musical shoulders with great solo artists such as Clark Terry, Louie Bellson, Ray Brown, John Handy, Max Roach, Bill Watrous, Bill Evans, Kenny Burrell, Bob Brookmeyer, Freddie Hubbard, Slide Hampton, J.J. Johnson and Jon Faddis.

In those days, the students met on Monday before the Festival, and by Thursday night the kids would perform at the traditional pre-Festival barbecue. One year, Schamber recalls, they played "at Macy's," at a party in the stereo/TV section of the store. "A little warm-up" he says, "for Sunday afternoon." Yet in spite of what some critics found to be the high school students' "positively frightening professionalism," problems continued to arise. Popular flugelhorn artist Chuck Mangione's request for a wide range of equipment, including tympanies, was forwarded to Lyons, who neglected to inform Schamber, who was in charge of preparation for the 1974 Sunday afternoon performance of Mangione's commissioned piece. Faced with the composer's wrath, Schamber replied, "Nobody told me a thing." Although the kids were familiar with some of Mangione's hit tunes, the score he presented them resembled a map of the New York City subway system, or a collage composed of chicken tracks. "I

looked at that and I thought, 'My God, I don't even think I could read it,'" Schamber says today. Yet the kids played the piece well.

Then came Art Pepper. A superstar on alto sax, Pepper was a former heroin addict braced, at this time, by large doses of methadone. Showing up late for his first clinic at the college, he stood on stage for half an hour playing a B-flat scale, put his horn in his case, and walked away. On Saturday morning, the day of All-Star Band auditions, Pepper constructed a twelve-bar blues passage impossible for *anyone* to play. Auditions began at one o'clock and, with forty-five to fifty hopefuls waiting in the wings, could last no more than five minutes. However, when the first contestant couldn't play the twelve-bar lick, Pepper insisted on showing him how. Hastily constructed thirty-second auditions were being held in other rooms, while the implacable Pepper continued giving thirty-minute saxophone lessons. Furious band directors from all over the state phoned on Monday morning, wondering why their kids hadn't been properly auditioned.

The Festival ran through a succession of musical directors for "the kids" throughout the Seventies: Herb Patnoe, Ladd McIntosh, Don Schamber, Jack Wheaton, Rich Matteson. In 1977, a woman of contagious energy (who sincerely believed that "music is the soul of a child" and the best way to reach kids) named Ruth Fenton joined the Board. She went to Yamaha and got a deal on a small instrument bank that consisted of five drum sets, a baritone saxophone, tenor saxes, alto saxes, and trombones. Because of these gifts, previously shy or reluctant high school jazz band directors were now increasingly attracted to a program that could benefit them directly.

Another key figure involved was esteemed guitarist Mundell Lowe. Co-founder of the Mobile Educational Jazz Festival in Los Angeles, Lowe also brought experience as an educator with him when he was hired to serve as musical director in 1983. He shares a "don't talk kids to death, just *show* them" philosophy with Bruce Forman. In 1983, at the urging of Lowe and Fenton, the Board decided that Festival funds needed to be redirected. An education committee was formed, and musicians such as drummer Vince Lateano, saxophonist Paul Contos, and trumpeter Bill Berry were hired to serve as traveling clinicians who would visit the range of schools in Monterey County. The kids had the utmost respect for Contos.

ABOVE: Among the best known and commercially successful graduates of the Festival jazz education program is pianist/composer/producer Patrice Rushen. She and Bill Evans played "Autumn Leaves" at the 1975 Festival. On the archive recording of this performance, while Evans seems to be calling, and playing, many of the rich improvisational shots, Rushen is very much there and makes you wonder, at times, just who is providing the fine notes. Trumpeter Clark Terry recalls Rushen as "one little girl who was so timid she was scared to come backstage, much less go on stage. She's a big name now."

They admired his playing ability, his teaching skills, and his humanity. "There was no negative anything from that man's mouth," Schamber says. "He was 110% dedicated to teaching kids how to play."

The first time the officially formed band of clinicians walked into Monterey High School, ten music students showed up. Yet from such a humble and perhaps temporarily discouraging beginning, the program mushroomed. Students learned to perform, not just study, a fairly sophisticated form of music. At the Youth Music Monterey summer jazz camp, sponsored by the Festival, small combo sessions instilled confidence, and also provided a healthy competitive edge. The kids respected – and adored – the clinicians, who were actual jazz musicians, not teachers. "Wow, this guy has an *album* out!" was a typical reaction.

Bill Berry, who has served as director of the California High School All-Star Big Band since 1981, says that the Festival had always hired a professional educator to lead the All-Stars, but in the Seventies, when that wasn't working out, Mundell Lowe advised that a professional musician be hired "just to see what happens." Lowe recommended Los Angeles big band leader Berry, and he's been there ever since. The process by which high school bands were selected also underwent a change. Tapes were still submitted by band directors throughout the state of California, but they were then sent, with no names attached, to North Texas State University, a school famous for its excellent jazz program. This move forestalled any cries of neglect or favoritism. Adjudicators in Texas picked the best ten bands and five combos and returned the tapes. The winning band and combo were selected at a competition held in April at the fairgrounds. This annual event has become almost as lively, as colorful as the September Festival itself.

ABOVE: *Everybody loved Dizzy Gillespie, and some – especially the "kids" who surround him here – idolized him.*

On Saturday, following a free clinicians concert, the top ten high school bands have their shootout. Members of rival groups stand off to one side, making comments such as, "Wow, that band exudes cool" or "This one is extremely egotistical." The Sunday individual All-Star auditions provide further color. Sax and trombone contestants lean against the cement block wall of a motel across the street from the Festival office, testing their chops. Parents and young hopefuls picnic on the back of pickup trucks or atop drum cases. Signs direct one to the "Sight Reading Room" or "Small Combo Warm-up." At the rhythm section competition, a continuous foursome – piano, bass, drums and guitar – plays while percussion judge Vince Lateano officiates. Contestants replace one another frequently and – "Okay," Lateano calls, "take it from letter B-33" – just jump into the chart.

In 1987, nineteen members of the Mon-terey Jazz Festival's California High School All-Star Big Band, together with Berry and Lyons, flew to Japan for an unofficial tour. Then, in 1989 the All-Star Band performed at the first annual Monterey Jazz Festival held in Noto (a peninsula in western Japan where Nanao, Mon-terey's sister city, is located and where, in the city of Wakura, the Festival has been held and the students have performed for the past nine years). The group rehearses for two days in Monterey and then takes off. On the road in Japan for two weeks, they can test their chops. After a lay-off of more than a month, the band has a week to rehearse before the Sunday afternoon appearance at the Monterey Jazz Festival. Berry brings all new music to this final rehearsal session, "but at least I know the band, or *most* of the band, by then," he says.

What started out as "Jazz Today and Tomorrow," a Sunday afternoon devoted to kids, has produced many fine professionals.

The list of All-Star graduates includes trumpeter Stacy Rowles, alto saxophonist Matt Catingub, Emmit Green (who played with Art Blakey's Jazz Messengers), pianist Eddie Mendenhall, saxophonist Craig Handy, saxophonist Dave Koz, and trumpeters Rebecca Frank and Tanya Darby. You can match a host of names up with the big bands they've worked with: Steve Mortenson (Glenn Miller), Danny House (Count Basie), Anders Swanson (Ray Charles), Donny McCaslin (Carla Bley), Luis Bonilla (Gerald Wilson), David Krimsley (Gerald Wilson), Mary Fettig (Stan Kenton), Joe Alessi (New York Philharmonic). The list goes on and on.

Some of the more successful professionals were products of a special program piloted by jazz educator Herb Wong, who once referred to the Festival as "a unique hidden curriculum" for jazz education. Acknowledging that Lyons, early on, included community college bands in afternoon concerts, Wong says Lyons later missed the boat. When he was establishing a jazz program for elementary school children (starting in kindergarten), Wong approached Lyons to lend financial support, but the general manager nixed the idea. Ten years later Lyons called and said he'd heard a fine young group of junior high school kids from Berkeley. "Oh really?" Wong replied, "what's the group?" "There's a kid named Peter Apfelbaum. He's about thirteen. Fourteen maybe. And there's a kid who's a little older, maybe a year, Rodney Franklin." Wong replied, "Jimmy, *those* are the kids I called you about when they were five to seven years old!" Both Apfelbaum and Franklin appeared at the Festival with the Berkeley High School Jazz Combo in 1975.

Both Bill Berry and Bruce Forman acknowledge the challenge of working with kids who have by no means grown up in a jazz-centered universe, but one in which many other forms of popular culture are more persuasive, and a readily available context for the music does not exist. "I always try to include at least one Basie, Herman or Ellington tune," Berry says of his work with the All-Stars, "because these bands are no more, and these kids are never going to get a chance to play that music, unless they get it now."

"Jazz is a language," Forman says. "Without having heard it, you can't speak it. Jazz is played on the same instruments as other music; it uses the same notes, but the nuances, the inflections, the dialects, the vocabularies are different. Most of the kids have never really *heard* this new language," Forman adds. They just try "to play it off a piece of paper." Consequently, he spends much of his clinic time performing for them: to let them know what their parts could sound like. "And then I give them the tools to do it themselves."

By 1992, a full-scale Monterey Jazz Festival educational program was in place. Success on a strictly local level was apparent. Whereas there had never been a single student from Monterey County in the All-Star Band, by 1994 there were ten. "When we started out as clinicians," Bill Berry says now, "we just made it up as we went along, as you would with a band; but the program kept growing and growing and growing, until now it's the most unique thing in the country." Stella LePine, education program coordinator since 1985, represents the Festival at national conventions. If she mentions some of the problems she has had with teachers, their indifference or resistance, the others say, "Are they *crazy*? We'd *kill* for a program like that."

Above the documented successes, LePine's personal rewards are even more vast, as they are for many involved. "I not only have my own five kids," she says, "but I've got a thousand more," an extended family of young jazz musicians she's watched grow up from eleven and twelve-year-olds to "you know, *big* kids," she says. They send cards at Christmas, and some, like pianist Matt Sagan, now an educational coordinator himself, stop to visit out of both friendship and gratitude for the Festival's early inspiration in their lives.

"I'm most proud of the jazz education aspect of the Festival," Jimmy Lyons said in 1992, when he stepped down after thirty-five years as general manager. The legacy of what he created continues to this day.

BELOW: Benny Green first appeared at the Festival as a fifteen-year-old pianist in the California High School All-Star Big Band. As early as the fourth grade he'd been part of an elementary school jazz program started by Dr. Herb Wong. Hearing his peers perform music he'd previously only associated with the faces of Thelonious Monk and Charlie Parker on record covers made an impact on him, as did looking up to older kids, such as Peter Apfelbaum. "I saw the level he was at as being the mountain top," Green says, "and that gave me a strong impetus to strive to move forward." Green's father stressed the importance of deciding whether jazz was going to be a hobby or something he wanted to dedicate his life to. By the time Green was a freshman at Berkeley High School he was ready, despite his young age. "I just knew that this was what I wanted to do and that was all that mattered," he says. "I thought that when I played in the All-Star Band at the age of fifteen, it would be my one and only shot at the Festival." Yet he returned in 1994 with the Ray Brown Trio, and in 1997 with his own group. OPPOSITE: Pianist Kito Gamble was first featured at the Festival with the Berkeley High School combo in 1991. Critic Scott Yanow recalls that performance as "quite remarkable." Everybody else sounded "like they were fifteen years old," but Gamble played a solo on "Take the 'A' Train" that made her sound "professional . . . a major discovery."

FRESH FACES

Throughout the years the Festival was dominated by familiar faces – thirteen veteran artists appearing a total of one hundred thirty-nine times – performances by new and more adventurous talents took a back seat, restricted to about one or two a year. No matter how fine the music of the veterans was, the menu became increasingly lopsided in favor of the known, and even die-hard fans began to yearn for something more, a less shopworn musical experience. Before he moved to Monterey from the East Coast in 1974, jazz DJ/die-hard Monterey Jazz Festival fan David Gitin attended the rival Newport festival, where he heard classic jazz clarinetist Pee Wee Russell team up with Thelonious Monk. There, Dizzy Gillespie and James Moody came on stage and jammed with blues exponents James Cotton and Muddy Waters. "I once heard folk singer Pete Seeger sing 'Summertime' with saxophonist Bud Freeman," Gitin says. "You had a sense," he adds, "that anything could happen at that festival."

In 1960, the Monterey Jazz Festival pledged to unite musicians who ordinarily wouldn't, or didn't, get to perform together, and promised to introduce new artists, rather than play it safe with an endless parade of name attractions. By 1975, when Gitin attended his first Monterey event, such aspirations had pretty much gone by the wayside, although there were occasional attempts to bring together disparate artists. A 1980 encounter between pianist John Lewis, violinists David Harrington and John Sherba, Hank Dutt on viola, and Joan Jeanrenaud on cello – or a young and exciting Kronos Quartet – resulted in a performance of

ABOVE: Bobby McFerrin first brought his extraordinary vocal range (from falsetto to deep bass) and substantial creativity to the event in 1983. A Festival favorite, he would return in 1984, 1986, 1987 and 1995. OPPOSITE In 1977, David Friesen took the all-too-frequently noisy Festival audience by surprise, and delight, with his solo bass performance of an original composition, "Children of the Kingdom."

OPPOSITE: Ann Patterson's Maiden Voyage, a seventeen-piece all-female band founded in 1980, and hailed by writer Frankie Nemko as "a major phenomenon on the West Coast," performed at the Festival in 1984. Saxophonist Patterson was a regular with southern California big bands and with the group Four Winds. Maiden Voyage boasted such fine instrumentalists as trumpeter Stacy Rowles (an alumna of the California High School All-Star Big Band), drummer Jeanette Wrate, and trombonist Betty O'Hara, who also lead their own groups and enjoyed international reputations.

Lewis' "Variant for String Orchestra." The piece commenced with a cello drone, a minimalist base or undercurrent that Lewis danced atop with classical agility. Impressionistic, openly lyrical or romantic by turns, the work harkened back to early Festival commissioned pieces – most of which had disappeared over the years.

John Lewis also organized "Piano Playhouse" events. The first in 1973 featured Ellis Larkins, Billy Taylor and Toshiko Akiyoshi; and a similar joint venture in 1975 included Lewis, Marian McPartland, Patrice Rushen (who just three years before had been selected as pianist for the California High School All-Star Big Band) and Bill Evans. Because of the Festival crowd's by now customary intoxicated rudeness, McPartland cut her portion of this performance short, saying backstage, "Never again." And she meant it. Not only were fine contemporary players not getting invited, some of those making their first appearance – such as McPartland – were disenchanted by the experience and would not return.

On the positive side, some jam session sets were made up of unique, well-selected musicians and frequently offered a particular theme. In 1973, "Bird Night" honored the great Charlie "Yardbird" Parker. Supersax, a group of Los Angeles studio musicians – which included Warne Marsh and Jack Nimitz – performed ensemble transcriptions of Parker's indelible solos. They were followed by a first-rate aggregate of mostly Bird-alumni: Dizzy Gillespie, Max Roach, John Lewis, Milt Jackson, Ray Brown, Sonny Stitt and Frank Rosolino. A "Bird Night" jam session included Parker's "Moose the Mooche," on which these musicians were joined by tap-dancer Baby Lawrence. A playful riff ensemble, with Milt Jackson's vibes in the lead, gave way to smooth melodic Roach wire brushwork capped by Lawrence's fine clicks, tapped lines and a strong shuffle, spiced with Gillespie's sweet muted trumpet. "Let's swing it out!" someone called, and they all did, the piece closing with a fierce drum roll.

Roach, who had appeared at the first Festival, was returning after a hiatus of sixteen years. The long absence was the result of his intense and confrontational involvement with the Civil Rights movement throughout that period. How great it would have been to hear his seven-part "Freedom Now Suite" – critic Scott Yanow calls it "timeless protest – a gem" – at the Festival during the Sixties. Max Roach reflects now, "The whole attitude of that music

was different. Perhaps Jimmy was just dealing with *sound,* with instrumental music for its own sake." At the time, Lyons was decidedly not dealing with messages.

Given the admirable intention of pairing off performers who might not ordinarily play with one another, other giant jam sessions presented at the Festival were often too loose and crowded. The chemistry wasn't right; musicians seemed thrown together. At one session, a 1975 "Jazz Vignettes," musicians filled the stage – Belgium's "Toots" Thielemans, Sweden's Svend Asmussen, and Germany's Albert Mangelsdorff among them – and played "The 'C' Jam Blues." A reluctant Paul Desmond stood among the horde. Caught in the traffic jam, he declined to even attempt to compete for a solo slot until Clark Terry pushed him forward.

The Monterey Jazz Festival's solid international reputation relies as much on the large number of foreign musicians it has welcomed to its stage as it does the substantial body of renowned American musicians it has featured over the years. Fortunately, artists unfamiliar to American audiences continued to appear during a time that even die-hard fans were beginning to label "the repeat years." The Festival provided performances by groups or single artists from the Philippines, Canada, Cuba, Japan, Sweden, Belgium, France, England, Wales, Germany, Hungary, Israel, Ghana, Brazil, and the Virgin Islands. When Spanish pianist Tete Montoliu performed with bassist Red Mitchell, the *San Francisco Examiner's* Philip Elwood praised the much admired blind Barcelona pianist as "brilliant," citing his "fantastic technique and intriguing ideas."

1977: On the Monterey Jazz Festival's twentieth anniversary, thirty-five-year-old bassist David Friesen, performing with trumpeter Ted Curson's innovative group, amazed both fans and critics. Curson himself said of Friesen, "He's a genius. It's not a term I often use." Critic Grover Lewis called the bassist "astonishing," saying Friesen "scored a personal triumph." Friesen performed *alone* on bass, and did so before a customarily manic Friday night crowd who actually *listened.* Writer Ira Kamin noted that Friesen was not just appreciated but "adored." The bassist hung around the Festival for a couple of days, according to Kamin, didn't drink or smoke and talked of "spiritual things." Reflecting on this encomium, Friesen laughs. Was he, at the time, the Festival's resident

RIGHT: A 1984 saxophone summit brought together, left to right, Eddie "Lockjaw" Davis, Richie Cole, Benny Carter, Slide Hampton, Al Cohn, James Moody, Eiji Kitamura, Clark Terry and Ann Patterson. In 1979 a creative "all-star" idea turned sour. Dizzy Gillespie was featured in a simulated nightclub setting. A host of musicians sat around at small round tables, waiting for Dizzy to select them for solos. He repeatedly overlooked the exciting, young, up-and-coming alto saxophonist Richie Cole, whom the audience was anxious to hear. Cole finally just shrugged his shoulders and left. Lyons and Gillespie had a serious tiff over the slight, and the trumpeter didn't return to the Festival until the 1982 Silver Anniversary. Cole came back the next year – Lyons certain to make amends in this case – and with a vengeance. Honored with the title "Artist at Large," he appeared with vocal group Manhattan Transfer and the Tokyo Union Orchestra, and performed on Saturday night with his own group, Alto Madness.

guru? "I don't think so," he says. "Music *is* spiritual," he adds. Oddly enough, the only people to complain about Friesen's unique performance were musicians who did not regard the bass as a lead instrument. In 1978, Friesen returned for the All-Star Band rendering of his own compositions, but Lyons said, "No bass solo," and David Friesen would not come back to the Monterey Jazz Festival again until 1995.

1979: Woody Shaw was an exciting young player, just thirty-four at the time, one of the finest trumpeters of the 1970s and 1980s. After his Monterey appearance, critics were unanimous in their praise of his quintet. Zan Stewart, in a *Down Beat* article ominously entitled "Monterey: Is Change Long Overdue?," found the group "sizzling," yet mourned the fact that they were only given twenty minutes to play, while Moe Koffman's "tepid Canadian fusion outfit" got forty-five. Leonard Feather said the group offered "a whirlwind of tensely energetic solos." Yet again, the musician who provoked such enthusiasm was not asked back. Eleven years after he performed in Monterey, Shaw died in New York from injuries suffered when he was hit by a train.

1980: Two exciting and innovative performers showed up as the new decade began: pianist JoAnne Brackeen and trumpeter Freddie Hubbard. Brackeen was granted only a short set. Japanese drummer Motohiko Hino explored various time signatures behind the pianist's loose open intro, the piece turning to marshall striding mixed with Bach, witty, solemn, paradoxical; then an up-tempo romp. Unfortunately, the Festival audience, talking and partying throughout her set, seemed unwilling to accept the challenge of Brackeen's demanding music. Critic Conrad Silvert hailed her appearance as "a subtle touch of progressive programming." He praised her ability to fight off the indifference of the audience in order to make fine music.

Freddie Hubbard fared somewhat better commanding attention, although Jimmy Lyons had to correct a small Freudian slip when he announced Hubbard as "someone who is *near . . . new* to our stage," adding he wished to bring "*new* friends to you delightful people who make up our audience in Monterey." One undelighted member of that audience shouted back, "It's about time!" Hubbard's group featured fine young pianist Billy Childs, and from the clarion

call opening of "One of Another Kind," they were just that: Hubbard's "Flight of the Bumblebee" ascents and swashbuckling style prompting *Billboard's* Eliot Tiegel to proclaim Freddie Hubbard "warm and gracious and comical and a total gas."

1982: At the Festival's Silver Jubilee, an excellent quintet fronted by saxophonist Ira Sullivan and trumpeter Red Rodney somehow managed to slip in between the familiar wrinkles, or cracks and, in spite of mike problems, offered a medley combining such strange bedfellows as "Greensleeves" and John Coltrane's "Giant Steps," a free jazz version of "Just a Closer Walk with Thee," and young pianist Garry Dial's original work "For Frederick (Chopin) and Bill (Evans)." Evans died just before Festival time the previous year, so the piece possessed an added emotional boost or edge. This was the group's first, and only, appearance, leading critic James Liska to comment, "Red Rodney and Ira Sullivan hardly fall into the category of 'newcomer,' but to Monterey audiences they must be."

1983: A "Guitar Summit," inspired by and including a new musical director, Mundell Lowe, brought together the diverse and mutually stimulating talents of John Collins, Eddie Duran, Bruce Forman, Ron Eschete and former high school All-Star Steve Grenadier. Backed up by a first-rate rhythm section composed of Hank Jones, piano, Shelly Manne, drums, and Andy Simpkins, bass, the group swung out on "Broadway," taking solos by turns and providing both a unique blend and contrast of voices: Collins, a Nat "King" Cole veteran of fourteen years standing, laid-back and low; Forman, at twenty-seven, fast and fiery, already a passionate perfectionist, dynamic – in both his own and musical – personality; Lowe, by contrast, cool and compatible and articulate as a favorite uncle. Another inspired 1983 match-up was that of trombonist Phil Wilson and exciting young Japanese pianist Makoto Ozone. Ozone had attended Berklee Music College in 1980. His wealth of natural ability and impressive acquired technique established him as a master of the piano's full range of effects. Lowe had the foresight to recognize his talent early.

1986: Frank Morgan won a television talent contest at the age of fifteen, released his own album in 1955, and then disappeared for thirty

OPPOSITE: Bill Evans, one of the most influential pianist of the Fifties, Sixties and Seventies, made just two appearances at the Monterey Jazz Festival. During the first in 1970, his trio performed Evans' original pieces with the Oakland Youth Chamber Orchestra. His 1975 "Up with the Lark," accompanied by bassist Eddie Gomez, was a handsome construction that moved into steady waltz time, and contained a brightly innovative piano/bass exchange fueled by intense lyricism. San Francisco Examiner critic Philip Elwood wrote that Evans had "never been stronger nor more imaginative, running through astonishing creations with assurance and a firm touch."

ABOVE: The appearance of Michel Petrucciani in 1991, with Adam Holzman on synthesizer providing the extraordinary pianist with atmospheric background, was a Festival highlight. Arranger/ educator Don Schamber, who had introduced and directed the first Monterey County Honor Band that Sunday, remembers listening to Petrucciani and, when the pianist embellished a tango with inhuman speed and control, responded, "How does he do that?"

years, reemerging with the release of his *Easy Living* album with the Cedar Walton Trio in 1985. He spent the missing three decades in San Quentin as the result of heroin addiction. Morgan's debut, or discovery, performance at Monterey was extraordinary. A master of the entire jazz vocabulary (pinched tones, overt wail, deflated or abruptly designated notes), agile as Astaire, his playing imbued with all the warmth and confidentiality of a club vocalist, Morgan turned the common agony of "Love Story" into his own story and back into that of the audience again. In combination with Alto Madness artists Richie Cole and Charles McPherson, Morgan provided more than just a dash of the unexpected. He gave the crowd a taste of excellence, as he would the following year when he appeared with the Cedar Walton Trio for the next leg of his resurrection.

1988: J.J. Johnson, who once astonished his peers with his fluid phrasing on passages deemed impossible to play on trombone,

proved that, after a twenty-seven year absence from the Festival, he could still stun a crowd with his own brand of excellence. Johnson, who had not been back since his 1961 triumph with his original composition "Perceptions," kicked off Sunday evening with his own quintet, after appearing with Bill Berry's Big Band around midnight on Friday. The equally extraordinary eighty-three-year-old Benny Carter was forced to wait until 1:30 a.m. to play before a nearly empty house.

1989: With the exception of the return of Freddie Hubbard and an appearance by the Illinois Jacquet Band, the Festival's offerings were conspicuously lacking innovation. Allegiances were becoming divided, a Festival civil war was shaping up. One group of die-hard fans remained fiercely loyal to Jimmy Lyons and the mainstream fare the sell-out affair offered annually. Another, continuing to attend the event, grew increasingly discontented. They felt that not making use of the world's full range of available jazz talent was a crime. Some fans actually circulated a petition on a clipboard, gathering addresses and names in protest against stale programming. Others grew impatient for a long-awaited Messiah who would step in as general manager and immediately transform the Festival. The cynicism of a few was cruel. When Lyons was sidelined by a heart attack, one devoted fusion fan responded, "We're just a heartbeat away from Lee Ritenour."

1990: In response to the growing clamor for change, Lyons brought the commercially successful pop/jazz group Spyro Gyra to the Festival stage on Friday night. The group was lodged between the Festival house band's opening jam and young saxophone sensation Christopher Hollyday. "They should have been last," observed critic Scott Yanow, who questioned Lyon's assessment of the group's appeal. "The veteran people in the audience didn't like them." This was also a year Dizzy Gillespie came out to perform with Stan Getz. Spying a package of cigarettes in the ailing tenor saxophonist's back pocket, Gillespie extracted it and threw it into the audience. The well-meaning act proved futile, however. While Getz provided a memorable set with pianist Kenny Barron in 1990, he would die of cancer in June the following year.

1991: Pianist Chick Corea returned to the Festival for his first performance since his 1969 appearance with the Miles Davis Quintet. Featuring Dave Weckl on drums and John Patitucci on bass, Corea's Akoustic Band gave a stirring performance. Alto saxophonist Phil Woods was another highly individual performer returning after a long hiatus: in his case, twenty-nine years. He and his quintet performed well, providing "Just a Dream," from the Benny Carter songbook. After the set, as if to signify that he'd been slighted for too long, Woods walked straight past Jimmy Lyons in sullen silence.

Few as they were, not every attempt at innovation or bringing back neglected faces to the Festival came off well. Feeble attempts at surprise were rooted in a sentimentality that accompanied the Festival's notion of itself as a "family affair." Lyons' generous but lugubrious introductions of artists – "My dear friend, my very, very dear friend" – began to sound hollow, especially when applied to musicians he didn't know or had just met. In 1988, Lyons found a seven-year-old drummer who, after several false starts as far as sound check went, dazzled a

not-too-discerning crowd with his wind-up toy pyrotechnics. The previous year Lyons had presented a six-year-old torch singer, advertised as having perfect pitch. Two Los Angeles school teachers refused to get sucked into the sentimentality. Like hardened critics, the first sat back and commented, "What can she know, at six, about *love*?" The second responded, "and besides, she ain't got no perfect pitch."

By 1991, the Monterey Jazz Festival seemed to be running short of ideas. The occasional rare appearances seemed only to highlight fatigue and a lack of imaginative programming. A refrain hovering on the horizon for some time now carried beyond the carping of professional jazz critics. "Change" was inevitable, and even Jimmy Lyons, in declining health, realized that his term as general manager might well be over. "He was very open about it," Lyons' close friend and San Francisco neighbor Ernie Beyl says. Although he knew he would no longer be "boss," Lyons hoped to have a continuing elder statesman's role, and have a hand in choosing his successor. Ruth Fenton, in poor health herself (she would die at the age of sixty-three in 1991), longed to see Festival leadership transmitted into imaginative and competent hands. Working with student musicians who performed there, she made the acquaintance of Tim Jackson, manager of the very successful Kuumbwa Jazz Center in Santa Cruz. The Board, seriously considering Jackson's candidacy, also learned that Lyons – discovering, as many potential retirees do, that there's a distinction between contemplating that massive step and actually taking it – had pulled back.

"When the time came," Beyl says, "Jimmy was not ready for it, psychologically." According to Lyons' wife Laurel, "The Festival was his joy. Lose his baby? Well, it was his life. You might as well have hit him over the head." The word most people involved use to describe that situation is "tough." It was tough on Lyons to give up the creation that had become his entire life, tough for a newcomer to step into a position embraced by someone else for thirty-five years, and a tough decision to be made by the Board of Directors.

Nevertheless, they made it. In March of 1991, the Board announced that Jimmy Lyons would step down as general manager of the Monterey Jazz Festival, and that Tim Jackson would take his place.

ABOVE: Toward the close of the Eighties an increasingly large portion of the Festival audience, fatigued by shopworn sets by artists they loved but had heard again and again, welcomed the high-energy performances of musicians such as tenor saxophonist Illinois Jacquet, who brought his own band to Monterey in 1989.

VARIETY and SURPRISE

Tim Jackson's office reflects the evolution of the Festival itself. Definitely not slick or spiffy, it's uncluttered, tasteful, efficient, yet casual and comfortable. Relatively state-of-the-art sound equipment stands near the desk, while the past smiles down, or glances, from the walls: posters from recent Festivals; photographs of Miles Davis, Sonny Rollins, Herbie Hancock, Dizzy Gillespie with the famed cheeks puffed out, blowing not a trumpet but bubble gum – some artists still living, some dead.

Jackson has managed the highly successful non-profit Kuumbwa Jazz Center in Santa Cruz for more than twenty years. Charged with grant writing, fund raising, supervising volunteers, and booking artists, he stayed abreast of the current jazz world. Schooled on the blues at twelve, he discovered Miles Davis and John Coltrane while in high school and has remained committed to jazz and its history ever since. Jackson is an accomplished musician himself, on flute and saxophone, an artist whose performance schedule remains as active as time permits. The ease, or cool, with which he maintains competence, even his collegiate good looks coupled with a straightforward, no-nonsense manner, made him the perfect choice to rejuvenate the Monterey Jazz Festival.

When Jimmy Lyons stepped down as general manager in 1992, people – especially the press – lost no time exploiting the potential for Freudian high drama, even though, Jackson, who was thirty-seven at the time, was no Oedipal upstart supplanting his seventy-five-year-old "father" on the road to Thebes. If an era, a major part of the Festival's history, was

ABOVE: In 1993, McCoy Tyner's big band – which included such superior sidemen as Billy Harper, John Stubblefield, Steve Turre, and Bobby Hutcherson on vibes as a special guest – came to the Festival. Tyner, who appeared at the event in 1961 with John Coltrane's famous quartet, was scheduled to open Saturday night with his own group in 1974, but his plane was delayed in Chicago. When he finally arrived, he was not allowed to go on. His big band, a hit of the night in 1993, more than made up for the nineteen-year delay. OPPOSITE: In 1992 Gerry Mulligan brought the dignity and uncompromised musical inventiveness of time and experience to Monterey.

BELOW: The Festival's co-founder and general manager for thirty-five years, Jimmy Lyons; photographer and die-hard fan Will Wallace; and the event's second general manager, Tim Jackson. OPPOSITE: Pianist/composer Billy Childs first performed in Monterey at the age of twenty, with the Aldeberts in 1977. He was back again in 1980, with Freddie Hubbard's quintet. Childs credits Hubbard with schooling him as to how "to think on my feet, how to comp," how to put into practice and refine what he already knew in theory about the bebop language. Ten years later Childs returned with vocalist Dianne Reeves, with whom he had worked in his own group, Night Flight. In 1992, Childs appeared with his own quintet: Bob Sheppard, reeds; Walt Fowler, trumpet; Tony Dumas, bass; and Michael Baker, drums. "That was one of my favorite groups," Childs says. In 1994, the pianist/composer showcased his commissioned piece "Concerto for Piano and Jazz Chamber Orchestra."

passing, the temptation to view it as Greek mythology was all too alive and well. Coast Weekly's Jill Duman alluded to the myth of Pygmalion and Galatea, the "artist who breathed life into his creation and then must step aside and let it live." Yet given the heavy emotional investment of the party going out, and the one coming in, the transition was actually quite smooth.

Jackson swiftly put to rest whatever fear and anxiety some of the more zealous fans entertained about the Festival's future. Possessing a flair for phrase-making, he summed up his approach in one of his first public statements, "I'm an evolutionist, not a revolutionist." When a portion of the jazz-loving public gave a heavy sigh of relief, Jackson also declared that he would continue to offer "quality stuff with an accent on tradition as well as innovation" – a promise of something-for-nearly-everyone that he's made good on. Evolution not revolution. Innovation coupled with tradition. Both comfort and hope were embodied in these phrases, and they grew to be slogans.

The most reassuring indication of a smooth, not unduly abrupt nor startling transition was embodied in action not just words. Programming for the 1992 Festival was a joint effort, a major act of cooperation between Lyons and Jackson. The event coupled the former's favorite fare with the latter's insight into all that was out there in the jazz world, what Jackson called "what's happening with both established and up-and-coming artists."

On Friday night, the Festival got off to a fresh start with twenty-three-year-old Roy Hargrove's Quintet. At the time, trumpeter Hargrove was heralded as a hot, original, fiercely talented young lion. His mix of well schooled hard bop, assertive R&B, and even – on "You Don't Know What Love Is" – a touch of Chet Baker's sweetness at the close, left little room for the customary straggling of the first-night family reunion. Full of energy and hebetic exuberance, his quintet featured one of the most exciting young drummers around, Gregory Hutchinson, pianist Marc Cary and Antonio Hart on alto saxophone, all of whom were under twenty-five years of age at the time. The group made the 1992 opening set itself, as Tim Jackson had predicted, an "historical event." Even the sad old main arena, which houses the Main Stage, burdened with its legacy of horse shows, looked somehow bigger and brighter that night.

Sunday night reflected and paid homage to Lyons' preferences and thirty-five years of dedication. The Dave Brubeck Quartet, the Modern Jazz Quartet, Gerry Mulligan, and an all-star jam session featuring Louie Bellson, Slide Hampton, John Handy, Red Holloway, Jon Faddis, George Bohanon, and Bruce Forman – all of whom had played a significant part in past Festivals – were on hand to pay tribute to Jimmy Lyons. So were other musicians associated with the event's rich legacy: Herbie Hancock, Wayne Shorter, Ron Carter, Wallace Roney and Tony Williams in a special "Tribute

LEFT: *Symbolic of the new rich chemistry general manager Tim Jackson was providing, in 1995, a fine generational match-up featured Eddie Harris on tenor saxophone – a legendary improviser responsible for the first million-selling jazz single, "Exodus", who would die of cancer in November, 1996 – and John Scofield on guitar, a master of many forms of jazz.*

to Miles Davis;" Mark Naftalin and his Blues Revue featuring Charlie Musselwhite, Katie Webster, Buddy Guy and Junior Wells; vocalist Betty Carter, and a fine quartet that included veterans Kenny Burrell, Jimmy Smith, Grady Tate and Stanley Turrentine.

The event was a perfect blend, a unique match up of the long-sustained vision of the man stepping down and the general manager assuming his place. Jackson's taste was again reflected by the appearance, on the Main Stage, of exciting young pianist Billy Childs' group and the Lincoln Center Jazz Orchestra – the embodiment of tradition laced with innovation, and the likes of Wynton Marsalis serving as a sideman – performing the music of Duke Ellington.

Such rich fare was charged with additional emotion because of the changing of the guard. The Main Stage crowd got an extra-musical kick at the start when, just before Roy Hargrove's set, a tall lean man who seemed somehow very familiar stepped out on stage and said, "I'm Clint Eastwood . . . and I love jazz." The 1992 thirty-fifth annual Monterey Jazz Festival closed out as dramatically as it began, with what columnist John Detro described as "Jimmy weeping at the end. Lyons showed great dignity, courage and honest emotion." "No commercial," the former general manager said at the close, "just thanks and God love you."

One of Jackson's first announcements was his intention to resuscitate the practice of assigning commissioned works. Again, an original principle – item number two of the 1960 Festival statement: "Monterey avoids the hackneyed and the trite by commissioning new works by prominent composers who are exploring the new frontiers of jazz" – was alive and well. The Festival's continuity was being restored. Pianist/composer Billy Childs, who was making a strong name for himself as both performing artist and an originator of fresh and arresting music of his own, was a perfect first choice. Childs had performed at Jackson's Kuumbwa Jazz Center and one day, according to the pianist, "Tim just called me and said, 'I'm starting up the commission series again. I want *you* to do it.' *Wow*! It was a great honor." Already part of the Monterey legacy, Childs first appeared at the Festival in 1977, when he was twenty, as keyboardist with the Aldeberts, a group from Los Angeles.

Commissioned to create what he named

"Concerto for Piano and Jazz Chamber Orchestra," Childs had been listening to Paul Hindemith's "Concert Music for Strings and Brass," and came up with the idea of engaging nine violins, three violas, three cellos, two trumpets, two trombones, three French horns, a single bass and his own rhythm section. Nicole Paiement was selected as conductor. Full rehearsal sessions were limited, but Childs says he rehearsed "like crazy" with the rhythm section in Los Angeles, then flew up to the Bay Area for a session with the strings and brass. Tim Jackson had heard only bits and pieces of the work via the telephone. Childs is a dedicated composer who is likely to suddenly interrupt a phone conversation, find a chord sequence while you are on hold, cry out, "That's it!" and then resume the conversation without a break. On stage, the piece was as much of a surprise for Jackson as it was for the audience. An unqualified success, the concerto earned Childs a standing ovation.

It was a natural step from Billy Childs to the next commissioned artist, Maria Schneider. Although he declines taking credit for acquiring "the gig for her," Childs did suggest Schneider when Tim Jackson inquired about a work for the following year. *Down Beat's* Thomas Conrad described her commissioned piece as "one of the essential big-band recordings of the Nineties," noting that the composer/arranger has the potential to become "a major voice." By 1995, she was an inevitable choice for the work she named "Scenes from Childhood."

Not considering herself a "long form" writer, preferring pieces of twelve to thirteen minutes in length, Schneider decided to compose a suite she had contemplated writing for some time. It would incorporate scenes from her childhood – sequences not seen "from a distance," as she puts it, "but truly entering *into*" what she felt at the time. She drew up a list of possible sketches, a "long list of music I could write on for the next ten years." Then she began to play with these separate experience pieces, and came up with three distinct movements. The first, "Bomb Shelter Beast," is about childhood tension, growing up during what she describes as "the horrible Sixties," with the threat of nuclear war, watching fear-inducing news on TV each night, sleeping next to the bomb shelter her father built to preserve the family's lives, seeing "Gilligan's Island" interrupted by nuclear test runs and waiting for the next air raid drill. The sound of the latter "com-

OPPOSITE: In 1995, Tim Jackson arranged a spring press-preview party held at Yoshi's nightclub in Oakland, thus reestablishing another tradition that had been lost. The first Monterey Jazz Festival was previewed at a similar event held at the Fairmont Hotel in San Francisco in 1958. Introduced at Yoshi's, Maria Schneider, who would provide a commissioned piece for that year's Festival, expressed her excitement over the Monterey project because she realized that, in the United States ("Europe keeps me alive," she claimed, "not $15 gigs in New York"), most big bands were not playing original music. Schneider believes that her big band, the Maria Schneider Jazz Orchestra – which appears every Monday night at the Greenwich Village jazz club Visiones – is holding up genuine tradition. It does what the old bands did, which is play original music that – as she puts it – "speaks of the time honestly," not harkening back to bygone days but "just doing what we do now."

ABOVE: The great bassist Charlie Haden first appeared at the Festival in 1965, with San Francisco pianist Denny Zeitlin and Jerry Granelli on drums. In 1993 he returned with his Liberation Music Orchestra, performing with the Oakland Youth Chorus. Haden's aggregate included extraordinary sidemen Robin Eubanks on trombone; Nicholas Payton, trumpet; Javon Jackson and Joshua Redman, tenor saxophones; Amina Claudine Meyers, piano; and Paul Motian on drums. OPPOSITE: Tenor saxophone titan Sonny Rollins, who made just two previous Festival appearances – the first in 1958, the second in 1972 – returned for a triumphal Sunday night set in 1994. Rollins, who filled the stage with his personal and musical presence, gave an overpowering performance. "They all stayed," he exclaimed when he came offstage.

ing over the horizon" in a small plains town was, as Schneider recalls, "just eerie." Her "Bomb Shelter Beast" begins with that sound, played on a theremin by baritone saxophonist Scott Robinson. The sound "didn't come off so well" at Monterey. It sounded more like "a race car than a siren," she says, "the theremin is a very temperamental instrument."

The second movement, "Night Watchmen," is built on the discovery of sensuality, its awakening, what Schneider calls "wishing things," a desire to move ahead into new but alien areas that may prove dangerous. This section is made up of images of a nocturnal landscape in which watchmen at a flax plant on the outskirts of Windon, Minnesota, made their shadowy rounds. The last movement, "Coming About," for which she *literally* returned to her home state to gather impressions after a long absence, is, unlike the first two, focused on a settled state of mind, when she felt truly "free and had a genuine best-of-Minnesota feeling," completing or finding a center for the other two sections.

At an MCI-sponsored press conference and in her clinic session, Maria Schneider's compositional skills were matched by her wit and wisdom as a fully articulate spokesperson for her music. She confessed she dreads hearing a piece in rehearsal the first time, what Schneider calls "in the raw, and nobody knows how they're supposed to play it yet and you hear it torn apart." She admitted that she went through a stage of "panic" before the Festival performance. "I knew what Billy Childs wrote was absolutely stunning. I heard that on the radio and I thought, 'Oh, my God.'" A tough act to follow, but she did, handsomely. When, following the presentation of this work, fans flocked to her clinic, she mentioned Miles Davis, how his voice was present "from the lowest note to the highest" in his playing. "I feel strongly that the only thing you can do better than anybody else in this world," she said, "is to express yourself genuinely, to tell your own story. *Nobody* can imitate that."

A press preview party. Commissioned works. Clinic sessions and press conferences in the MCI press tent. "Tradition as well as innovation," or innovative tradition. Looking back on such healthy signs of renewal, on reintroducing what had worked well in the past and was instilling vitality into the present, Jackson says, "You play on the strengths of your festival. We've got forty years of history behind us; why

not play off that?" Jackson believes Monterey can offer programs other festivals can't simply because they haven't been around long enough. So Jackson takes advantage of the Festival's legacy. Why *not* present a commissioned work each year? Why *not* have as much access to the artists as possible, both musically *and* verbally? "It doesn't make any sense," Jackson adds, "*not* to do it."

With that in mind, Jackson inaugurated an artist-in-residence program in 1994. Musicians such as Dizzy Gillespie and Gerry Mulligan had served as "roving artists" in the past, but this made the weekend-long presence of such artists official. Saxophonist Bob Mintzer and pianist James Williams shared that first slot. A highly versatile reed player, Mintzer led his own fine big bands, had worked with Jaco Pastorious and the Thad Jones-Mel Lewis Orchestra, and joined the popular Yellowjackets in 1991. The Yellowjackets appeared at the Monterey Jazz Festival in 1992 and 1996.

James Williams' Contemporary Piano Ensemble – which featured the sumptuous talents and additional forty fingers of Donald Brown, Geoff Keezer, Harold Mabern and Mulgrew Miller – kicked off the 1994 show, and kicked it into high gear. Their set closed with a Williams' original, "That Church Thing," which found the five pianists circling the *four* instruments they'd been at work on, clapping hands and leading a gospel parade.

Williams explains that for clinic sessions, such as the one he conducted at Monterey on Sunday afternoon in 1994, he tries to get a general idea of, in his terms, "the level of artistry" of his audience. If students say they are "advanced," he responds, "That's interesting, because I'm not yet an advanced student myself." His assumption is *everybody* is an "intermediate, and we work from that point on." The essential element for Williams is learning "how to *listen* to each other," not just on the surface but "intimately." There's a major difference between *hearing* and listening, and genuine listening, which is an art form in itself, is the key to the art of jazz. Williams stresses two other factors. One: jazz is a metaphor for life, it prepares you for life; and two: jazz musicians have a responsibility to take the music out to audiences, *everywhere*, just as an evangelist would his or her religion. Playing in an ensemble, artists have to work well with other people, even some they may not *like*, in order to achieve a common *sound* or goal. Ultimately,

Williams teaches, "the music is the star of the show. The music stands tall."

In 1996, Jackson took the "tradition of innovation" approach one step further by offering reenactments or recreations of Jon Hendricks' "Evolution of the Blues," originally performed in 1960 (and again in 1972), and Lalo Schifrin's "Gillespiana," originally performed in 1961. Jon Faddis stepped in for Dizzy Gillespie in the latter. Tapping into the Festival's Golden Age, Jackson conveys his admiration for that "alive and creatively vibrant time" when you could "put together a Miles Davis and a John Coltrane and a Thelonious Monk and a Charles Mingus and a Duke Ellington and a Louis Armstrong – *all* those people in one place, at one time!" From 1993 through 1995, Monterey Jazz Festival fans were treated to programs that offered the talents of musicians such as Bobby Watson, Charlie Haden's Liberation Music Orchestra, Ruben Blades, the Brecker Brothers, the McCoy Tyner Big Band, Dorothy Donegan, Joe Henderson, the Ray Brown Trio, Max Roach and M'Boom, Shirley Horn, Sonny Rollins, Gene Harris, John Scofield, Eddie Harris, Stephane Grappelli, Chick Corea, Charlie

Hunter, Toots Thielemans, and Steve Turre and Sanctified Shells. In 1994, Ornette Coleman returned to the Festival for the first time in twenty-seven years. The inventive strident sounds of Prime Time forced old guard Festival fans to abandon the arena, but spirited jazz columnist Wayne Saroyan howled with glee, "Leave! Leave!," relishing the evening's genuine musical variety and surprise.

A new Golden Age? Perhaps such an era, having established its near mythical identity, remains inviolable and cannot occur twice. Yet the players just cited hardly constitute a fall from grace. In awe of the past, standing in its shadow, we may fail to see the glory of what surrounds us, of what we are living *in*. Yet the continuity, the glory days, are a part of our living present: the variety and surprise restored. The Monterey Jazz Festival had reclaimed its supremacy, its reputation as one of the world's major jazz events. Indeed, some people complained that, now, there was almost too much fine music to choose from! Such an embarrassment of riches characterized the Festival's Golden Age, and now, in fresh contemporary dress, that age *has* returned.

BELOW: Fresh faces characterized the 1993 Festival. Two excellent musicians who had never appeared before were the Brecker brothers, Michael on tenor saxophone and Randy on trumpet, shown here assisted by guitarist Mike Stern. OPPOSITE: The real ambassador: in 1992, popular pianist Dave Brubeck returned for his tenth Festival engagement.

OUT ON THE GROUNDS

The 1992 program put together by Jimmy Lyons and Tim Jackson offered a healthy mix of the familiar and the new, a sort of seamless variety. To fans eager for immediate change, Jackson may have appeared to be a far more reasonable figure than the long-awaited Messiah they'd counted on. Yet if the Main Stage still bore the imprint of Lyons' veteran performers, Jackson immediately left the stamp of his own personality out on the grounds. A close look at what was happening outside the Main Stage, on the Garden Stage and in the Night Club that year, discloses a host of fresh unfamiliar faces and truly innovative music – even avant-garde. At the time, you could feel the change in the air, and it reflected major changes taking place in the world of jazz at large.

Sandwich boards set up before the Garden Stage, an area with open-air seating tucked behind the midway food booths, and the Night Club, an intimate setting and comfortable walk several yards down the way, boasted the names of Peter Apfelbaum and the Hieroglyphics Ensemble, the New World Trio, Nancy King and Glenn Moore, Zen Blend, the Fowler Brothers, and the Larry Vuckovich International-Multicultural Quintet.

The New World Trio, featured on the Garden Stage, included violinist India Cooke, cellist Kash Killian, and drummer Eddie Marshall. The group, with its unusual instrumentation, combined gypsy exuberance and chamber music exactitude on jazz classics such as "Bemsha Swing" and Cooke's original "62383." Later, at the Night Club, Marshall would propel his own solid group, containing young lions Peck Allmond on trumpet and Kenny Brooks on

ABOVE: Dmitri Matheny, right, and Dave Ellis, products of the vital Berkeley, California, jazz scene, perform on the Garden Stage. OPPOSITE: Vocalist Ann Dyer, shown here performing in Dizzy's Den, is attracted to dynamics, to meaningful contrasts she finds missing in some jazz performances. She likes to find material that dramatizes many different aspects of life, not just what she calls "romantic pining" – although she says, "I like that too." In 1996 Ann Dyer and the No Good Time Fairies offered songs on every topic from Beatles psychedelia to urban jitters to the bucolic pleasures of a song written by drummer Jason Lewis, "New England Cowboys."

ABOVE: Although in 1992 Peter Apfelbaum's Hieroglyphics Ensemble may have produced what struck some fans as unprecedented sounds, its leader was no stranger to Monterey. He had been a member of the 1975 prize-winning Berkeley High School combo. In 1992 Apfelbaum put together a band that included two drummers, two electric basses, a violinist and bassoon. The result was dissonant orchestral opulence, a rhythmic bouillabaisse with messages buried in prodigious volume. One piece incorporated lines from poet Dylan Thomas: "The hand that signed the treaty/bred a fever, and famine grew/and locusts came." BELOW: The Night Club hosted a Sunday afternoon "conversation" with pianist Herbie Hancock in 1996. The event – held before a capacity crowd enthralled by Hancock's reminiscences, reflections and revelations – was moderated by writer Al Young. OPPOSITE: In 1994, Columbia Records hosted a live recording session in the Night Club that featured up-and-coming talent such as (shown here) David Sanchez and his quartet. Billed as a "Columbia Jazz Jam," the event also included the Black/Note Quintet from Los Angeles, vocalist Nnenna Freelon, and the Terence Blanchard Quartet with vocalist Jeanie Bryson.

reeds. Another group, the Fowler Brothers, offered witty free jazz, making use of what jazz writer Scott Yanow described as "a quirky sense of humor." Innovation, humor, exuberance. Out on the grounds, fresh sounds and new soundings on old standards were very much in the air. So was a sense that previously overlooked musical directions were no longer just on the horizon but had finally become a part of the Festival's total fabric.

Vocalist Kitty Margolis was indicative of the change. Having appeared at Monterey in 1989 and 1990, she embraced the pivot year 1992, and would return again – by then an extremely popular performer who drew long lines of fans waiting to get into her Night Club set – in 1994 and 1996. She was a singer who would make Festival fans forget their fix on the Sarah Vaughans and Carmen McRaes of the past. No less a figure than Lionel Hampton had reinforced this impression when he said, "At last the search is over. The next great jazz voice is Kitty Margolis."

Festival audiences were willing, and eager, to follow her in whatever musical direction she might go. Referring to that audience, the singer confides that, "corny as it may sound," you *live* "for that love that comes back to you." Nothing is as amazing as what Margolis calls "the circle of energy" that, on a good night and with a good crowd, is created between stage and audience. "It's the biggest high there is," she claims, "and it's *legal*."

Part of a new breed that has managed to combine academic training (she majored in visual and environmental studies at Harvard) with good *street smart* musical experience (she also played guitar in a western swing band), Margolis is as straightforward, confident, spunky and vibrant off the bandstand as she is on it. Critics have praised her for taking chances, for the risks she assumes scat singing and reinterpreting jazz standards. "I think that's part of my personality," she says, "I think you really sing *who you are*. I've always been a person who liked a thrill, so to me, nothing is more thrilling than scatting or improvising."

The jazz press has linked Margolis to two other divas, Ann Dyer and Madeline Eastman, who've performed at Monterey, both products of an active Bay Area jazz scene Berkeley writer Dan Ouellette has described as "one of the most important spawning grounds in the country for female jazz vocalists." Ann Dyer has a comprehensive background, having studied dance at Mills College. The sets she performs with her group, the No Good Time Fairies, seem almost *choreographed* in a manner that she claims is not conscious, but probably just *there*. She calls it a "release of conscious editing." Standing very still in the spotlight in the traditional vocalist's mode would require censoring, so Dyer prefers a natural "very kinesthetic" approach that allows all aspects of her personality to surface. Madeline Eastman is hailed also for her risk-taking, her range of repertoire, her ability to move easily from up-tempo scat singing to sensuous bal-

ABOVE: Dr. Lonnie Smith at the Hammond B3 Organ. In 1995, a fourth venue opened directly across from the Night Club. Christened "Dizzy's Den," it was host to a barn-burning organ summit, a tribute to Johnny "Hammond" Smith that featured Lonnie Smith, Ronnie Foster, Bill Heid, and Larry Goldings rotating on two instruments. Guitarist Bruce Forman and tenor saxophonist Eddie Harris fanned the flames. Fans literally ran down the midway to witness the spectacle, once the news got out.

RIGHT: Guitarist Charlie Hunter brought his trio, which featured Dave Ellis on tenor saxophone and Scott Amendola on drums, to the Night Club in 1994. Having attracted considerable national attention, this exciting young group returned in 1995 to perform on the Jimmy Lyons Stage.

OPPOSITE: The 1993 Festival featured a Night Club "conversation" between veteran guitarist/banjoist Danny Barker, shown here, and bassist Milt "The Judge" Hinton. The event, billed as "Living Jazz History," drew a capacity crowd. Barker, eight-four at the time, and Hinton, eighty-three, whose jazz paths first crossed in Chicago in the mid-Thirties, delighted the audience with stories that spanned the years – and miles – from New Orleans to Monterey.

lads. Eastman first appeared at Monterey in 1987, and has returned three times, in 1991, 1993 and 1995. "We take turns," Ann Dyer, who first appeared at the Festival in 1991 and returned in 1994 and 1996, says – adding that as friends, the one who is not performing in a particular year "comes down and keeps the other one company."

"You see just about equal numbers of men, women, old people, young people, black people, white people," Margolis says of her visits. Jazz festivals in Europe are full of Europeans. Jazz festivals in Japan are full of Japanese. Jazz festivals in Australia are full of Australians. But the Monterey Jazz Festival, Margolis claims, "is full of just *everybody.*"

Other groups with what Berkeley critic Dan Ouellette calls "distinctive dialects" and "ever evolving idioms" have appeared on the Festival grounds: Alphabet Soup; Glenn Spear-

man's Double Trio, with ROVA saxophonist Larry Ochs; drummer Josh Jones' Hueman Flavor, Dmitri Matheny, Mingus Amungus, the Charlie Hunter Trio, Rhythm & Rhyme Featuring Wayne Wallace, Eddie Marshall & New Flavor, Tom Peron/Bud Spangler Quartet, Dogslyde and Mark Levine's Quintet.

"I think we've always done a good job of integrating local and regional artists," Jackson claims, "and we've been lucky to have great artists to draw from in the area." The Festival, starting from night one in 1958, has always included a wealth of local Monterey talent: Jake Stock and the Abalone Stompers, Jackie Coon, Jan Deneau, Dave Clay, Bill Jackson, Bob Phillips, Roger Eddy, Terry Miller, Andy Weiss, Helcio Milito and Weber Drummond, John Cortes, Kenny Stahl, drummer/vocalist Dottie Dodgion and Ace Hill.

In 1995, a fourth venue opened directly across from the Night Club. Christened "Dizzy's Den," it hosted an organ summit, a tribute to Johnny "Hammond" Smith. Also featured that first year at Dizzy's Den were Joyce Cooling & Person to Person; Bobby Bradford, Vinny Golia and Kimara; and San Francisco pianist Denny Zeitlin, returning after an eleven-year absence, coupled with bassist David Friesen, also back after a seventeen-year hiatus.

Jackson is attempting to dispel an attitude "that you had the Main Stage and then you had all the other stages." In his quest for equalization of venues, he has gone so far as to excise the term "Main Stage" from future Festival publicity. "I want to make this *just* the Monterey Jazz Festival," he says. "There's no *main* anymore, because that gives the impression everything else is secondary." The problem came home when he himself performed at the 1989 Festival, appearing in the Night Club. Having been seriously involved with both musical production and performance for years, Jackson found the venue "an afterthought" when it came to production values. Consequently, he has invested a lot of time, and money, into equalizing venues, from how they look to how they sound to overall design and seating. In 1994, the Main Stage was re-christened the "Jimmy Lyons Stage." A fifth setting, the Coffee House Gallery, situated on the midway between the main arena and the Garden Stage, opened in 1997.

Added to the musical variety, and clinics on the grounds, Jackson has inaugurated a series of talks or "conversations." On Sunday afternoon, in 1994, Dr. Herb Wong held a "Jazz Legend" session with Max Roach in the Night Club. Asked back to the Festival for the first time in eleven years, Roach says today that, at the time, he was concentrating on an evening performance with his group M'Boom, dedicated, in Roach's words, to preserving "the definite musical personality" of American jazz, a totally orchestral percussion ensemble that employs techniques and rhythms developed in this country. Consequently, he was somewhat reluctant about the distraction of a public interview session. Wong said, "Come on Max;" Roach replied, "All right; it's not going to hurt. It's just going to be a few minutes." Two hours later, Roach, a natural raconteur, had the sizeable audience in the palm of his hand listening to firsthand accounts of nights playing with Charlie Parker – who gave other players intricate harmonic designs verbally, then just looked over at the drummer and said, "*You know what to do!*" – to Dizzy Gillespie playing a trumpet riff during a symphony performance of Stravinsky's "Petrouchka" at the first Monterey Jazz Festival.

In April of 1994, the man most responsible for starting the legendary Festival, Jimmy Lyons, died at the age of seventy-seven. A panel discussion entitled "Remembering Jimmy," moderated by the Festival's former publicity director, Ernie Beyl, celebrated the co-founder's life at the September Festival. Yet testimony reached far beyond the fairgrounds. "We clicked together," longtime musical director John Lewis said. "We had good chemistry." Veteran staff member David Murray said, "His love of music and his jazz 'family' – that's what motivated him." Reflecting, Lyons' wife Laurel says, "What can you say except that the Festival is magnificent? The continuity of it. The perfection of it. Jimmy got great joy out of everything he did."

Lyons was lauded for his loyalty to friends, for sticking to his guns in preserving mainstream jazz (when others sought elsewhere – in pop, rock, fusion or avant-garde music – for greater stimulation), for helping to develop the concept of the jazz musician as a serious artist, for initiating the jazz education program of which he became so proud, and for restoring a full musical life to forgotten performers such as Earl "Fatha" Hines, Helen Humes and Jimmy Witherspoon. It would be difficult to list Lyons' accomplishments in order of importance. Faced with the task of doing so, Ernie Beyl says, "Maybe they're all number one."

ABOVE: In 1993, pianist Sumi Tonooka brought a trio featuring Rufus Reid on bass and Ben Riley on drums to Monterey for Main Stage and Night Club performances. Tonooka also presented a clinic in the Night Club that focused on what she calls "the very mysterious process" of composition. Tonooka disclosed that the act commences, for her, with "something very personal . . . a picture of someone I know or a very vivid scene in my mind." She illustrated the process with "Phantom Carousel," a tune inspired by a vision of a carousel on a mountain top shrouded in mist, the voices of children "in the air" but no children present. The piece, technically, was also inspired by a six-note Egyptian scale. Like Festival "conversation" sessions, informal yet highly informative clinics gained in popularity between 1993 and 1997.
OPPOSITE: "The Judge," Milt Hinton: the dean of jazz bassists, avid photographer, record producer, jazz historian and first-rate raconteur.

CONTINUITY
and CONTINUATION

Drummer Joe Morello appeared at the first Monterey Jazz Festival. Forty years later, one of his former students, Joe Green, was president of the Festival Board of Directors. In 1959, a fourteen-year-old Jim Costello was not permitted to work at the Monterey Jazz Festival, even though his sister Molly, just fifteen was. Costello recalls that, because of the chill on stage, his sister lent her red usher's cape to vocalist Annie Ross, and then, the following year – when Costello *was* permitted to work – found a Board member's coat for Sarah Vaughan. Four decades after that first event, Jim Costello was a member of the Board of Directors. Such continuity is a significant part of the full story of the Monterey Jazz Festival.

Joe Green started coming to the Festival in 1963. A high school student at the time, Green played drums in a San Francisco Bay Area rock band, and listened to good blues on Alcatraz Avenue in Oakland, "a syncopated sort of rhythm that made me go home and practice a lot harder." His favorite jazz drummers were Joe Morello, "a great musical drummer," and Shelly Manne, whose subtle licks he tried to reproduce on his own kit. At that time he had just one ambition in life: "to be a great drummer!" Ironically, Joe Green played a major part in the transformation of the Monterey Jazz Festival's educational program in the Eighties, and served as chairman of the educational committee until four years ago, when he became Board president.

He "studied" at Bop City, a San Francisco after-hours club where Green first heard Thelonious Monk. While a serious music student at Foothill College, Green met John

ABOVE: High-profile vocalist/guitarist George Benson, whose 1976 Breezin *was the best-selling jazz album of all time, brought his successful mix of musical genres to Monterey in 1996. Shown on bass is Stanley Banks. OPPOSITE: One of the highlights of 1994 was the appearance of the Ray Brown Trio with special guests Milt Jackson, J.J. Johnson and Christian McBride. Sixty-eight-year-old Brown, right, was paired off with twenty-two-year-old McBride in a stunning bass duet. Brown recalls, "Tim Jackson just asked me, 'Why don't you do something alone with Christian?' And I said, 'Okay, but you know this crowd.'" The crowd loved it. "Once in a while you get fooled up there," Brown adds.*

RIGHT: In 1997, Festival fans were shocked and saddened to learn of the death at the age of fifty-two of the great drummer Tony Williams. Williams first appeared – at the age of seventeen – with the Miles Davis Quartet in 1963, returned with his own group, Lifetime, in 1969, and paid homage to Davis alongside Herbie Hancock, Wayne Shorter, Ron Carter and Wallace Roney in 1992.

Handy, the saxophonist sitting in with Green's fellow Foothill Jazz Ensemble friends, giving them "some direction and helping us with the bebop that we were all trying to do our best to emulate well." Green studied with Morello later on, and also Louie Bellson, who occasionally served as a clinician at Foothill. Joe Green is now a CPA whose office walls are lined with Festival posters from over the years, and reflect the legacy of his mentors, all of whom figured prominently in Monterey Jazz Festival history.

As Board president, Green brings the same enthusiasm and dedication he once brought to drumming to pet jazz education projects. And, as an accountant, he understands the figures, the cost. Proud of the fifty-thousand-dollar National Endowment of the Arts grant the Festival received in 1995, he calls the Arts Plus program, an innovative arts-centered curricula for which the money was granted, "a platform, a pilot project." Traditional disciplines such as English, history, and jazz as an art form will no longer exist in isolation, but meet and become one. Writer Al Young and singer Mary Anne Randl were recruited to implement courses at Monterey High School. Young brought the exciting singer/guitarist Adlai Alexander, with whom he had presented a "Words & Music" set at the 1995 Monterey Jazz Festival. The school session focused on the Harlem Renaissance. Randl presented a session on "Women in Jazz." Green is also excited about a 1997 Festival collaboration with Berklee College of Music in Boston to establish the Jimmy Lyons Scholarship, a full-tuition, renewable award given each year to an outstanding student musician from Northern California.

Looking back on many years of active affiliation with the Monterey Jazz Festival, Green recalls a pre-Festival Thursday night barbecue held in the days when musicians, arriving early in town, liked to just come and hang out. Green was sitting at a picnic table under a large oak tree that served as a canopy, a fire blazing in a large metal pot to supply warmth, and he suddenly realized that his idol, drummer Shelly Manne, was sitting to one side of him, regaling another Board member and fellow musicians with entertaining stories. "I went home dancing on a cloud," Green says today. "Sweetheart!" he cried to his wife when he walked in the door, "You can't believe who I sat next to tonight!"

Board of Directors member Jim Costello

admits he had the good fortune to grow up a "jazz brat." His uncle, Peter Breinig, brought Jimmy Lyons to Big Sur. Costello's father served on the Board from 1964 until his death in 1982, at which time his son, after acting one year as a gate supervisor, came on the Board himself. During the restless Sixties, Costello, then a student at the University of California at Davis – "the calm campus, where some of us felt left out," he claims – brought Ralph Gleason to the school to speak. Gleason, "a genius-type person" in Costello's eyes, was, at the time, branching out from jazz to rock and free speech. Costello says that Gleason's pen, and conversation, always let you know right where he stood, and that Gleason had enormous influence on Jimmy Lyons in those days.

Possessing a rich legacy of Festival history, Costello finds today's audience has a respect for the music that was lost during the more extreme *party* era, that long stretch of time when people came, in Costello's words, "because they'd been coming every year." He mentions the "repeat years," one portion of the audience loyal to familiar faces such as Woody Herman and Sarah Vaughan, another portion "there for the party and they didn't care who was coming." The audience is younger than before, less inclined to open drug use – "although the bar tab keeps on rolling" – nearly studious when it comes to listening to the music. Some of these new fans, whom Costello suspects may be classical music appreciators converted to jazz, anticipate indoor concert listening conditions at the event, and are very intolerant of the residue party atmosphere. Even the Saturday afternoon blues show has grown tamer. A few die-hard fans complain that they are no longer allowed to dance, but "*we aren't stopping them*," Costello says. "A lot of people who were dancing in the aisles thirty years ago just can't do it anymore." Mobs of people who used to hang out by the Main Stage have been dispersed. Costello recalls, during the years he was in charge of the gates, people attempting to get into the arena by way of displaying hundred dollar bills wrapped around their fingers. He kept track one year, calculating that he had turned down six-thousand dollars in potential cash bribes from those who didn't have tickets.

Costello claims a portion of the impetus behind the now extensive jazz education program was attracting young people to the music. If the Festival hadn't actively worked to

ABOVE: "The thing that's always been great about Monterey," general manager Tim Jackson believes, "is that it's always been the result of one person's artistic vision, and the Board has always been supportive of that." Jackson attempts to take "all the factors into consideration," to consult others, and then select, on his own, what is "the best, most pleasing artistically and enjoyable show." Some critics may have questioned Jimmy Lyons' artistic vision in the Festival's later years but, according to Jackson, that vision "had a lot of integrity to it." It stood the test of time. As for making artistic decisions on his own, Jackson says, "I like the feeling that ultimately there's no one else to blame. You sink or swim with your own ideas."
OPPOSITE: Howard Johnson's six-man tuba consort Gravity! kicked off Friday night in 1996. They proved that the tuba, once considered a strictly down-in-the-cellar subordinate instrument, was capable of full orchestral range, deep feeling, and could truly swing.

build an audience for the future, the event ran the risk of dying out. Mary Piazza was convert- ed to jazz when, attending an early rock 'n roll concert as a high school student in the late Fifties, she saw an older jazz saxophonist shuf- fle on stage as a warm-up act. He was wearing a pork pie hat, and his name was Lester Young, one of the immortals – now known as "Pres" – of the jazz world. Today, the Festival office coor- dinator, Piazza believes that young fans who come to hear Charlie Hunter's group are also favorably exposed to veteran performers they don't know, and become converts to jazz in the same way she did. A new family of fans with diverse tastes is coming into being.

The thirty-ninth annual Monterey Jazz Festival was kicked into high gear, in 1996, by a six-man tuba group, Howard Johnson's Gravi- ty! Johnson and his cohorts succeeded in showing a first-night crowd that this previously down-in-the-cellar instrument had amazing resilience and could, when called upon to do so, soar to the skies in trumpet fashion. Also on the Jimmy Lyons Stage that night, twenty- seven-year-old Joshua Redman gave ample evidence of why his appeal is riding high. He granted the audience the legacy of a tenor sax- ophone cadenza people are still talking about. Total weekend fare ranged from recreations of "Gillespiana" and "Evolution of the Blues," to a blues show that featured Taj Mahal, Otis Clay and Irma Thomas, the latter billed as "The Soul Queen of New Orleans." The popular Yellow- jackets appeared, along with an equally crowd- pleasing George Benson. Sunday night's

Jimmy Lyons Stage offerings included Cedar Walton's commissioned piece "Autumn Sketch- es." The superb pianist/composer was ably assisted in this premiere by a string section from the Oakland East Bay Symphony and excellent sidemen Roy Hargrove, Vincent Her- ring, Ralph Moore, David Williams and Marvin "Smitty" Smith. On Sunday night, Jon Jang astounded audiences with his sextet's beautiful and powerful interpretation of Charles Mingus' "Meditations on Integration," the piece enhanced by the otherworldly erhu sound of Cheng Jiebing. Herbie Hancock's quartet, with Dave Holland on bass and Craig Handy on saxophone, was joined by artists-in-residence Redman and Hargrove, who wrapped up the night in grand style.

Music offered elsewhere, on the Garden Stage, the Night Club and in Dizzy's Den was just as rich and, for the taste of some fans, maybe even more imaginative and challenging. Appearing were: Billy Mitchell, Dann Zinn, the Hy-Tones with Paul Contos; a Latin Friday night featuring Claudia Gomez, flutist Ali Ryerson with Helcio Milito, and Claudia Villela; Mike Vax's Alice Arts Center Jazz Orchestra, trum- peter Leroy Jones, and the Ethnic Heritage Ensemble. Highlights were – according to critic Scott Yanow – "the stunning technique, light touch and non-stop creativity" of pianist Jessi- ca Williams and the Dave Douglas String Group, which Yanow found "the most memo- rable band of the night . . . eccentric, witty, and colorful, swinging in its own way while looking towards the classic Ornette Coleman Quartet

and Albert Ayler." Such prodigious fare was off-set by clinics provided by Redman and Har-grove, a joint *Down Beat/Jazz Journalists* Asso-ciation sponsored "Blindfold Test" with Howard Johnson, moderated by Berkeley writer Dan Ouellette, and a capacity crowd "conversation" held between Herbie Hancock and writer Al Young. All in all, 1996 held out a sumptuous feast that prompted critic Scott Yanow to claim that the Festival "continues to get better year-by-year."

Such comprehensive programming bears the personal stamp of general manager Tim Jackson, who believes "a festival is about as many different styles of jazz as there are." Jackson believes so strongly in providing diver-sity that he claims he'd be disappointed if the audience liked everything, suspecting that the Festival was catering to a single segment at the expense of others. In 1997, the Monterey Jazz Festival will be providing music at five different venues, and if fans can't find *something* they like there, Jackson jokes, "the sixth option is to go *eat*," or go shopping at one of the many booths that line the midway.

The fairground that Louis Lorillard, tobacco magnate, jazz enthusiast and co-founder of the Newport Jazz Festival visited as a consultant before 1958 and, found had "no equal as a festival site" has, according to Jack-son, "pretty much maxed out." Yet, "there's no sentiment from anybody on our Board of Direc-tors to move this Festival somewhere else," Jackson says. Even if new technology has, from a production standpoint, pretty much passed the fairground venue by, the Festival can still boast what Jackson calls "that magical setting; Monterey is an incredible slice of the world." Jackson feels that the Monterey Jazz Festival and its ideal site once served as a "prototype, a model for jazz festivals in gener-al" – programs presented in "a concentrated period of time, all in one space." The trend for festivals today is to spread out – both geo-graphically and with regard to time frame. Jackson acknowledges the advantages of such formats, but "the great thing about the Mon-terey model is you can set up a total jazz vibe for that complete time period." You come through those gates and you go into another world for a few days. It's intense, it's fun, and the site has never lost its mystique.

When Jackson and Jim Costello approached Clint Eastwood, a dedicated jazz fan who lives in nearby Carmel, with the idea

of producing a compact disc and video cele-brating the fortieth anniversary of the Festival, the actor/producer replied, "I'm only in if it can be fun. Let's not get too damn serious." East-wood insightfully recalled an event from the first Festival in 1958. An airplane disrupted Dave Brubeck's performance – and airplanes still disrupt performances each year, a tradi-tion fans anticipate and applaud – and Brubeck immediately switched and swung into a few bars of "Wild Blue Yonder." That sponta-neous response, Eastwood believes, set the tone for the entire Monterey Jazz Festival. The Festival remains an event that sets high musi-cal standards, provides amazing historical performances, and pleases people from all over the world. And yet the Festival has never lost sight of the fact that it's supposed to be *fun*.

A major international event, the Monterey Jazz Festival has managed to perpetuate itself and, at the same time, remain festive and spontaneous, just as its founders hoped it would. It remains an entity that goes beyond individual performance, an event that embraces and unites grounds, concerts, musi-cians, patrons and atmosphere. Whatever its origins – religious quest or mom-and-pop store, or perhaps the two uniquely combined – the Monterey Jazz Festival and its family have ful-filled one of the oldest and highest aspirations of humankind: an extended family that circles the globe. And that family speaks a common language: the joyous language of jazz.

ABOVE: Gerald Wilson first appeared at the Festival in 1963, leading an All-Star Festival Orchestra that included Harold Land, Teddy Edwards, Jack Nimitz and Joe Pass. He directed a tribute to the music of Jimmy Lunceford in 1976, composed and conducted a com-missioned piece, "The Happy Birthday Monterey Suite," on the occasion of the Festival's twentieth anniversary in 1977; and brought his Orchestra of the '80s to the silver anniver-sary in 1982. Wilson returned as artist-in-residence, and con-tributed a commissioned piece to celebrate the event's fortieth birthday.

FESTIVAL PERFORMANCES AND PERFORMERS

Texas blues singer Mance Lipscomb made his only Festival appearance in 1973.

NOTE: The following does not pretend to be a definitive list of *all* Monterey Jazz Festival performers and performances over the past forty years. That task might easily require a book in itself – complicated by the fact that, on occasion, performers may not have arrived to perform (on dates contained in official programs) or, given the flexibility of sets, might sit in unannounced (or not at all). The following *selective* list was derived from Festival programs, financial archives, and magazine and newspaper reviews of actual performances.

Performances are grouped chronologically, and within each year by day and time, from Friday night to Sunday night. Beginning in 1983, the Festival scheduled full-time simultaneous performances on the Main Stage and at numerous venues elsewhere on the grounds. Performances at the grounds stages are shown after the Main Stage sets. The names of groups – or individual performers – are cited, with vocalists or significant sidemen in parentheses. Masters of ceremonies and conductors or directors are acknowledged. Names of original pieces are cited in italics, followed by the composer's name. Names of specific programs, thematic pieces or panels are also italicized, with the names of performers or participants placed in parentheses. Because of the difficulty of doing so accurately, pieces specifically commissioned by the Monterey Jazz Festival are not set apart from original works contributed by artists themselves; both are cited as original works.

1958

FRIDAY NIGHT: Dizzy Gillespie, M.C.; Burt Bales and the Dixie All-Stars; Jake Stock and the Abalone Stompers; Lizzie Miles; Louis Armstrong and the All-Stars (Velma Middleton); Ed Zubov Band (outside stage); Grace Stock (intermission piano).

SATURDAY AFTERNOON: Betty Bennet; Brew Moore and Dickie Mills Quintet; **Jazz Forum** (Louis Armstrong, Dizzy Gillespie, Ralph J. Gleason, John Lewis); Leroy Vinnegar Quartet (Teddy Edwards); Mastersounds; Med Flory Band; Mel Lewis-Bill Holman Quintet; Rudy Salvini Band; Pete Rugulo conducting Salvini-Flory combined band; Shelly Manne and his Men (Russ Freeman, Herb Geller); Virgil Gonsalves Sextet; Claude Gilroy Quintet and Ed Zubov Band (outside stage).

SATURDAY NIGHT: Buddy DeFranco; Buddy Montgomery; Cal Tjader Sextet; Dizzy Gillespie Quintet; Ernestine Anderson with Gerald Wiggins; Gerry Mulligan Quartet (Art Farmer); Jimmy Giuffre Three (Bob Brookmeyer, Jim Hall); Max Roach Quintet (George Coleman, Booker Little); Sonny Rollins; The Modern Jazz Quartet.

SUNDAY AFTERNOON: Dave Brubeck Quartet; Gregory Millar conducting the Monterey Jazz Festival Symphony; works by Werner Heider and Andre Hodier; **Jazz Impressions of Eurasia** by Brubeck; The Modern Jazz Quartet; **Toccata for Jazz Percussions and Orchestra** by Pete Phillips (Max Roach).

SUNDAY NIGHT: Mort Sahl, M.C.; Benny Carter; Billie Holiday; Dave Brubeck Quartet (Paul Desmond); Harry James Orchestra; Jimmy Giuffre Three; **Western Suite** by Guiffre.

1959

FRIDAY NIGHT: Lambert, Hendricks and Ross, M.C.'s Chris Barber Band; Earl "Fatha" Hines; George Lewis New Orleans Band; Jimmy Witherspoon with Monterey Jazz Festival All-Stars; Lizzie Miles.

SATURDAY AFTERNOON: **The Big Three** by Ernie Wilkins (Ornette Coleman, Coleman Hawkins, Ben Webster); works by Benny Golson, J.J. Johnson, John Lewis and Quincy Jones; Coleman Hawkins and Orchestra; J.J. Johnson and Orchestra; Ornette Coleman and Orchestra; Woody Herman and the All-Stars (Charlie Byrd, Zoot Sims).

SATURDAY NIGHT: Cal Tjader Quintet; Lambert, Hendricks and Ross; Modern Jazz Quartet; Woody Herman and the All-Stars (Ernestine Anderson).

SUNDAY AFTERNOON: Brass Ensemble performs new works by Werner Heider, Andre Hodier, J.J. Johnson, John Lewis; Buddy Collette; **Symphony for Brass and Percussion** by Gunther Schuller; Modern Jazz Quartet; Paul Horn.

SUNDAY NIGHT: Count Basie and Orchestra (Joe Williams); Lambert, Hendricks and Ross; Oscar Peterson Trio; Sarah Vaughan.

1960

FRIDAY NIGHT: Andre Previn Trio; Gerry Mulligan Orchestra (Zoot Sims, Bob Brookmeyer); Helen Humes; J.J. Johnson; Lambert, Hendricks and Ross.

SATURDAY AFTERNOON: **New Music**, conducted by Gunther Schuller; Festival String Quartet; John Coltrane Quartet; Ornette Coleman Quartet.

SATURDAY NIGHT: **Suite Thursday** by Duke Ellington; Duke Ellington Orchestra; Jimmy Rushing; Julian "Cannonball" Adderley; Lambert, Hendricks and Ross.

SUNDAY AFTERNOON: **Evolution of the Blues Song** by Jon Hendricks (Miriam Makeba, Big Miller, Odetta, Jimmy Witherspoon, Lambert, Hendricks and Ross).

SUNDAY NIGHT: Lambert, Hendricks and Ross; Louis Armstrong All-Stars; Modern Jazz Quartet; Montgomery Brothers/Monk, Buddy,Wes; Ornette Coleman Quartet.

1961

FRIDAY NIGHT: Duke Ellington, M.C.; Jimmy Rushing and Big Miller; John Coltrane Quartet (McCoy Tyner, Eric Dolphy, Wes Montgomery); **Modern Mainstream Set** (Dizzy Gillespie, Johnny Hodges, Ben Webster); Terry Gibbs Big Band.

SATURDAY AFTERNOON: **Ellington Carte Blanche**; Duke Ellington Orchestra.

SATURDAY NIGHT: Duke Ellington, M.C.; Carmen McRae; Dizzy Gillespie Quintet; George Shearing Quintet with J.J. Johnson and Festival Brass Choir; Joe Carroll and Dizzy Gillespie.

SUNDAY AFTERNOON: **Gillespiana** by Lalo Schifrin; Gunther Schuller, conductor (Dizzy Gillespie); **Perceptions** by J.J. Johnson (Dizzy Gillespie).

SUNDAY NIGHT: Duke Ellington, M.C.; Dave Brubeck Quartet (Paul Desmond); Duke Ellington and Orchestra; Odetta.

1962

FRIDAY NIGHT: The Swingers (Earl "Fatha" Hines, Ben Webster, Benny Carter, Rex Stewart, Bill Harris); **The Blues Song** (Helen Humes, Jimmy Rushing, Jimmy Witherspoon); **The New Continent** by Lalo Schifrin (Benny Carter, Dizzy Gillespie); Workshop Orchestra (Benny Carter, Mel Lewis, James Moody, Phil Woods, Bill Perkins, Conte Candoli, Red Callender); Earl "Fatha" Hines, intermission piano solos; Stan Getz Quartet.

SATURDAY AFTERNOON: **Salute to the Sax** (Benny Carter, Paul Desmond, Stan Getz, James Moody, Phil Woods, Gerry Mulligan, Ben Webster).

SATURDAY NIGHT: Dave Brubeck Quartet (Paul Desmond); Gerry Mulligan Quartet; Lambert, Hendricks and Bavan Trio; Quincy Jones and the Monterey Jazz Festival Orchestra; Ted Curson; Vince Guaraldi Trio.

SUNDAY AFTERNOON: Dizzy Gillespie Quintet; **The Relatives of Jazz** (Bola Sete, Francisco Aquabella; The Virgin Island Steel Band; Yaffa Yarkoni).

SUNDAY NIGHT: **The Real Ambassadors** by Dave and Iola Brubeck (Louis Armstrong, Dave Brubeck, Carmen McRae, Lambert, Hendricks and Bavan); Dizzy Gillespie/ Monterey Brass Ensemble; Jeanne Lee and Ran Blake; Louis Armstrong and His All-Stars.

1963

FRIDAY NIGHT: Gerald Wilson and the All-Star Festival Orchestra (Joe Pass, Harold Land); Jack Teagarden and Pee Wee Russell (Sleepy Matsumoto, Gerry Mulligan, Joe Sullivan); Lambert, Hendricks and Bavan; Miles Davis Quintet (Herbie Hancock, Tony Williams); The Modern Jazz Quartet.

SATURDAY AFTERNOON: The Andrews Sisters and the Gospel Song; The Drums of Ghana; The Elmer Snowden Trio; Turk Murphy and Earthquake McGoon Band; Joe Sullivan; Festival Swing Band (Teagarden, Russell, Mulligan).

SATURDAY NIGHT: Gerald Wilson and the All-Star Festival Orchestra; Gerry Mulligan Quartet; Helen Merrill; Jon Hendricks; Thelonious Monk Quartet (Charlie Rouse).

SUNDAY AFTERNOON: Gerald Wilson and the All-Star Festival Orchestra; Gerry Mulligan; Laurindo Almeida and Modern Jazz Quartet; The Drums of Ghana; Thelonious Monk.

SUNDAY NIGHT: Carmen McRae, M.C.; Dave Brubeck Quartet (Paul Desmond); Dizzy Gillespie Quintet (James Moody); Harry James and His Orchestra; Jimmy Witherspoon.

1964
FRIDAY NIGHT: Art Farmer Quartet; Gerry Mulligan; Jon Hendricks and Company (Gildo Mahones Trio); Miles Davis Quintet; Pee Wee Russell All-Stars (Buck Clayton, Vic Dickenson, Bud Freeman).

SATURDAY AFTERNOON: **The Blues -- Right Now** by Jon Hendricks (Hank Crawford, Lou Rawls, Big Joe Turner, Joe Williams, "Big Mama" Willie Mae Thornton, Homesick James).

SATURDAY NIGHT: Carol Sloane; Duke Ellington and His Orchestra; Gerry Mulligan; Horace Silver Quintet (Joe Henderson); Jon Hendricks and Company; The Modern Jazz Quartet.

SUNDAY AFTERNOON: **Meditations on Integration** by Charles Mingus; Charles Mingus Sextet; Festival Workshop Ensemble (Buddy Collette, Director); Thelonious Monk Quartet.

SUNDAY NIGHT: Dizzy Gillespie Quintet; Jon Hendricks and Company; Vince Guaraldi and Bola Sete Quartet; Woody Herman and 1964 Herman Herd.

1965
FRIDAY NIGHT: Dizzy Gillespie Quintet; Gil Fuller with the Monterey Jazz Festival Orchestra (Harry "Sweets" Edison, Clark Terry); Louis Armstrong All-Stars; Mary Stallings.

SATURDAY AFTERNOON: **Rebel Voices**: Charles Mingus Octet; Denny Zeitlin Trio (Charlie Haden); **Abstract Realities** by Russ Garcia; Gil Fuller with the Monterey Jazz Festival Orchestra; John Handy Quintet.

SATURDAY NIGHT: Anita O'Day; Duke Ellington and His Orchestra; Earl "Fatha" Hines; Gil Fuller and the Jazz Festival Orchestra (Dizzy Gillespie).

SUNDAY AFTERNOON: **Trumpets** (Dizzy Gillespie, Clark Terry, Rex Stewart, Henry "Red" Allen); **Angel City Suite** and **On the Road to Monterey** by Gil Fuller (Dizzy Gillespie); **Saint Martin de Porres** by Mary Lou Williams (Monterey Jazz Festival Singers).

SUNDAY NIGHT: Cal Tjader Quintet; Dizzy Gillespie Quintet; Ethel Ennis; Harry James New Swingin' Band (Buddy Rich).

1966
FRIDAY NIGHT: Count Basie Orchestra; Dave Brubeck Quartet (Paul Desmond); Gerry Mulligan; Gil Evans and the Monterey Jazz Festival All-Star Orchestra (Ray Brown, Elvin Jones).

SATURDAY AFTERNOON: **Blues All the Way**: Jon Hendricks, host; "Big Mama" Willie Mae Thornton; Jefferson Airplane; Jimmy Rushing; Jon Hendricks Trio; Memphis Slim; Muddy Waters Band; Paul Butterfield Blues Band (Mike Bloomfield); Shakey Horton.

SATURDAY NIGHT: Bola Sete Trio; Cannonball Adderley Quintet (Joe Zawinul); Carol Sloane; Elvin Jones -- Joe Henderson Quartet; Gil Evans and the Monterey Jazz Festival Orchestra (Cannonball Adderley, Ray Brown, Booker Ervin, Elvin Jones, Gerry Mulligan, Bola Sete).

SUNDAY AFTERNOON: Charles Lloyd Quartet; Don Ellis 21-Piece Workshop Orchestra; Gil Evans and the Monterey Jazz Festival Orchestra; John Handy Quintet.

SUNDAY NIGHT: Carmen McRae; Denny Zeitlin Trio; Duke Ellington Orchestra; Randy Weston Sextet.

1967
FRIDAY NIGHT: Dizzy Gillespie Quintet; Illinois Jacquet Quartet (Louie Bellson, Ray Brown, John Lewis); **Jazz Violin Conclave** (Svend Asmussen, Ray Nance, Jean-Luc Ponty); The Don Ellis Orchestra.

SATURDAY AFTERNOON: B.B. King; Big Brother and the Holding Company (Janis Joplin); Richie Havens; T-Bone Walker; The Clara Ward Singers.

SATURDAY NIGHT: The Woody Herman Orchestra (Mel Torme); The Ambrosetti Quintet (Nils-Henning Orsted Pederson); The Modern Jazz Quartet;.

SUNDAY AFTERNOON: Gil Melle and the Electronic Jazz Quartet; **Concerto for Orchestra No.** 2 by Miljenko Prohaska; Ornette Coleman Quartet; **Memorial to Billy Strayhorn** by Louie Bellson; The Don Ellis Orchestra; The Gabor Szabo Quintet.

SUNDAY NIGHT: Carmen McRae; Earl "Fatha" Hines Quartet; The Dizzy Gillespie Quintet; **Concerto for Herd** by Bill Holman; Woody Herman Orchestra.

1968
FRIDAY NIGHT: Mel Torme, M.C.; Count Basie Orchestra; Craig Hundley Trio; Gary Burton Quartet; Oscar Peterson Trio; The Dektet (Rudy Salvini).

SATURDAY AFTERNOON: **Masters of the Blues** ("Big Mama" Willie May Thornton; B.B. King; Jimmy Rushing; Muddy Waters; Vince Guaraldi Quartet).

SATURDAY NIGHT: Carmen McRae, M.C.; Don Ellis Orchestra; The Gabor Szabo Quintet; The Modern Jazz Quartet; The Third Wave (George Duke Trio)

SUNDAY AFTERNOON: **A Generation of Vibers** (Gary Burton, Bobby Hutcherson, Milt Jackson, Red Norvo, Cal Tjader); **Jazz Suite on the Mass Texts** by Lalo Schifrin (Orchestra and Choir; Tom Scott); Gabor Szabo Quintet.

SUNDAY NIGHT: Billy Eckstine, M.C.; Cal Tjader Quintet; Dizzy Gillespie Quintet; Earl "Fatha" Hines Orchestra; Earl "Fatha" Hines Quartet (Budd Johnson, Oliver Jackson); Palinho Quintet; Tom Scott Quartet.

1969
FRIDAY NIGHT: Modern Jazz Quartet; Peanuts Hucko -- Red Norvo Quintet; Sly and the Family Stone; Tony Williams Lifetime (John McLaughlin).

SATURDAY AFTERNOON: Bobby Bryant and Festival Soul All-Stars (Little Esther Phillips); Buddy Guy Blues Band; Roberta Flack and Her Trio; The Lighthouse.

SATURDAY NIGHT: Monty Alexander, intermission piano; Bobby Bryant and Monterey Jazz Festival Soul All-Stars; Joe Williams; Miles Davis Quintet (Wayne Shorter, Chick Corea); Thelonious Monk Quartet.

SUNDAY AFTERNOON: **Dido's Lament** and other pieces by John Lewis; **Progression in Tempo** by Gunther Schuller; **Rise and Fall of the Third Stream** by Bill Fischer (Festival Orchestra with Josef Zawinul); **Strings for Monterey** (Jean-Luc Ponty with Bobby Bryant); works by Ponty, Ron Carter, Cedar Walton, Nat Adderley; Modern Jazz Quartet with Los Angeles String Quartet; Nat Adderley; The Fourth Way.

SUNDAY NIGHT: Cannonball Adderley Quintet; Jean-Luc Ponty; Sarah Vaughan; The Buddy Rich Band.

1970
FRIDAY NIGHT: Alan Copeland Singers; **The Afro-Eurasian Eclipse** by Duke Ellington (Duke Ellington Orchestra); The Modern Jazz Quartet; Tim Weisberg Quintet.

SATURDAY AFTERNOON: Johnny Otis Show (Little Esther Phillips, Jimmy Rushing, Big Joe Turner, Eddie "Cleanhead" Vinson, Ivory Joe Hunter, Charles Brown).

SATURDAY NIGHT: Cannonball Adderley Quintet; Joe Williams; Slim Gaillard, Slam Stewart; Woody Herman Orchestra.

Earl Newman designed his first Monterey Jazz Festival poster in 1963 and sold it for one dollar on the midway. The following year, Newman's official poster featuring his stylized drawing of a saxophone player drew an X-rating from the mayor of Monterey, who asked shopkeepers to withdraw it from their windows. The three hundred posters that were printed immediately became collector's items and the mayor was deemed by many to be a prude. In the years that followed, Newman's hand-printed posters became synonymous with the celebration of jazz in Monterey. All fifty of his designs are included in the Smithsonian collection and have been recognized internationally as symbols of the American jazz scene. Newman, who now resides in Summit, Oregon, calls the Festival "a celebration – something I've always felt thankful to be part of."

FESTIVAL PERFORMANCES AND PERFORMERS

Trumpets ascending: Dizzy Gillespie, right, and his protègè Jon Faddis shared the stage in 1978.

SUNDAY AFTERNOON: Bill Evans Trio; **Circle Suite** by William Fischer (Gabor Szabo); Modern Jazz Quartet; Prince Lasha's Firebirds (Bobby Hutcherson, Sonny Simmons); **Tensity** by David Axlerod; **Experience in E** by William Fischer and Josef Zawinul; Oakland Youth Chamber Orchestra (directed by Denis de Coteau; Cannonball Adderley Quintet).

SUNDAY NIGHT: Duke Ellington, M.C.; Buddy Rich Orchestra; Gabor Szabo Sextet; Hampton Hawes Trio; Leon Thomas and Black Lightning; Sonny Stitt and Gene Ammons.

1971
FRIDAY NIGHT: Carmen McRae; Dave Brubeck Quartet (Gerry Mulligan); Louie Bellson All-Star Band (Harry "Sweets" Edison, Joe Pass, Ray Brown).

SATURDAY AFTERNOON: **Kansas City Revisited**; Al Hibbler; Jay McShann's Kansas City Six; Jesse Price Blues Band (Big Joe Turner); Mary Lou Williams.

SATURDAY NIGHT: Erroll Garner; Jimmy Witherspoon and Friends; John Handy/Ali Akbar Khan; Thad Jones – Mel Lewis Band.

SUNDAY AFTERNOON: **Jazz Today and Tomorrow**: California High School All-Star Big Band (Louie Bellson, Ray Brown, Clark Terry, John Handy); **Berlin Dialogue for Orchestra** by Oliver Nelson; McMinnville Oregon Twilighters; Ygnacio Valley High School Jazz Band.

SUNDAY NIGHT: **A Salute to Jazz at the Philharmonic** (Eddie "Lockjaw" Davis, Louie Bellson, Ray Brown, Benny Carter, Oscar Peterson, Zoot Sims, Bill Harris, Clark Terry); Oscar Peterson Trio; Sarah Vaughan.

1972
FRIDAY NIGHT: Elvin Jones Quartet; Modern Jazz Quartet; Stan Kenton Orchestra (conducted by Buddy Rich and Nat Pierce).

SATURDAY AFTERNOON: Jon Hendricks' **Evolution of the Blues** (Eddie "Cleanhead" Vinson, Jimmy Witherspoon)

SATURDAY NIGHT: **Giants of Jazz** (Art Blakey, Roy Eldridge, Al McKibbon, Thelonious Monk, Sonny Stitt, Clark Terry, Kai Winding); Herbie Hancock Septet; Joe Williams; Mary Lou Williams Trio; Sonny Rollins Quartet (George Cables).

SUNDAY AFTERNOON: Alan Locke High School Jazz Combo (Patrice Rushen); Bonita High School Band; California High School All-Star Big Band (Louie Bellson, Ron Carter, John Lewis, Oliver Nelson).

SUNDAY NIGHT: Cal Tjader Quintet (Dizzy Gillespie); Quincy Jones Orchestra; Roberta Flack.

1973
FRIDAY NIGHT: Buddy Rich and his Orchestra; Clare Fischer Quintet; **Piano Playhouse** (Toshiko Akiyoshi, Ellis Larkins, John Lewis, Billy Taylor); Pointer Sisters.

SATURDAY AFTERNOON: **Singin' the Blues**: Jon Hendricks, M.C.; Bo Diddley; Dave Alexander Trio; Eddie "Cleanhead" Vinson; **History of the Jazz Dance** (Baby Lawrence, and Others); Jimmy Rogers and His Chicago Blues Band; Mance Lipscomb.

SATURDAY NIGHT: **Bird Night**: Carmen McRae; Dizzy Gillespie and his Quintet; Modern Jazz Quartet; Supersax (Conte Candoli, Warne Marsh, Jack Nimitz); **Special Tribute to Charlie "Bird" Parker** (Ray Brown, Dizzy Gillespie, Milt Jackson, John Lewis, Max Roach, Frank Rosolino, Sonny Stitt).

SUNDAY AFTERNOON: California High School All-Star Big Band (directed by Ladd McIntosh, Max Roach, Clark Terry, Ray Brown, Bill Watrous); Corona High School Jazz Band; Grant Union High School Jazz Combo.

SUNDAY NIGHT: **Family Night** (Percy, Tootie and Jimmy Heath, Conte and Pete Candoli, Thad and Elvin Jones, Jackie and Roy Kral, Jimmy and Stacy Rowles, Stanley and Tommy Turrentine); Thad Jones – Mel Lewis Big Band (Dee Dee Bridgewater, Jon Faddis).

1974
FRIDAY NIGHT: **International Piano Forum** (Eubie Blake, Dillwyn Jones, George Shearing, Martial Solal); Monterey Jazz Festival Quartet (Richard Davis, Roy Burns, Dizzy Gillespie, Illinois Jacquet, John Lewis, Mundell Lowe, Gerry Mulligan); Sarah Vaughan; Toshiyuki Miyama and the New Herd.

SATURDAY AFTERNOON: Jon Hendricks, M.C.; Big Joe Turner; Bo Diddley; Dizzy Gillespie; Eddie "Cleanhead" Vinson; James Cotton Blues Band; Reverend Pearly Brown; Sunnyland Slim and the Blue Spirit Band.

SATURDAY NIGHT: Monterey Jazz Festival Quartet; Anita O'Day; Dizzy Gillespie Quartet (Clark Terry, Roy Eldridge, Harry "Sweets" Edison); **Guitar Summit Session** (Jim Hall, Michael Howell, Mundell Lowe, Joe Pass, Lee Ritenour).

SUNDAY AFTERNOON: California High School All-Star Big Band (Don Schamber Director, Ladd McIntosh Director, Dizzy Gillespie, Chuck Mangione, Gerry Mulligan, Clark Terry); Eagle Rock High School Band; Grant Union High School Combo; Lowell High School Concert Orchestra.

SUNDAY NIGHT: **A Latin Jam -- Inventions on Manteca** (Dizzy Gillespie, Toshiyuki Miyama and the New Herd; Mongo Santamaria, Clark Terry); Airto Moreira; Cal Tjader Quintet; Jerome Richardson.

1975
FRIDAY NIGHT: Barry Martyn and the Legends of Jazz; Helen Humes with Gerald Wiggins; **The Piano Playhouse** (Bill Evans, John Lewis, Marian McPartland, Patrice Rushen); Toshiko Akiyoshi/Lew Tabackin Big Band.

SATURDAY AFTERNOON: Bobby "Blue" Bland; Etta James and Friends; Sunnyland Slim; The Meters.

SATURDAY NIGHT: **Jazz Vignettes** (Svend Asmussen, Paul Desmond, Benny Golson, John Lewis, Toots Thielemans, Albert Mangelsdorff, Clark Terry); Chuck Mangione Quartet; Ed Shaughnessy Energy Force Big Band (Diane Schuur); Helen Merrill and Friends.

SUNDAY AFTERNOON: Berkeley High School Combo (Peter Apfelbaum, Rodney Franklin);California High School All-Star Big Band (directed by Don Schamber and Ladd McIntosh; Bill Evans, Benny Golson, John Lewis, Chuck Mangione, Pat Williams); Richmond High School Big Band; Oakland Youth Symphony Orchestra (directed by Denis de Coteau).

SUNDAY NIGHT: **Point of View** by John Lewis (Svend Asmussen, Monterey Jazz Festival Quartet, Hubert Laws); Betty Carter and Alfred "Chip" Lyles Trio; Blood, Sweat and Tears; Dizzy Gillespie Quartet (Cal Tjader).

1976
FRIDAY NIGHT: **A Tribute to Louis Armstrong** (Benny Carter, Doc Cheatham, Harry "Sweets" Edison, Dizzy Gillespie, Clark Terry); **The Music of Fletcher Henderson** (Bill Berry and the Festival All-Star Band; Benny Carter, Russell Procope); **The Music of Jimmy Lunceford** (Gerald Wilson and the Festival All-Star Band, Snooky Young); **A Tribute to Bebop** (Dizzy Gillespie Quartet, Benny Golson, Sonny Criss).

SATURDAY AFTERNOON: Berkeley High School Combo (Peter Apfelbaum); Reseda High School Jazz Band; Hollywood Fats Blues Band (Johnny Shines); James Cotton and Chicago Blues Band; Jimmy Witherspoon; Margie Evans; Queen Ida and the Bon Ton Zydeco Band; Seaside Bethel Baptist Church Choir; The Olympia Brass Band.

SATURDAY NIGHT: **The Music of Count Basie -- a Basie Retrospective** (Nat Pierce, Vic Dickenson, Harry "Sweets" Edison, Buddy Tate, Jo Jones); Olympia Brass Band; Helen Humes with Gerald Wiggins; **Commemorating the Duke** (Festival Orchestra directed by Bill Berry, Cat Anderson, Russell Procope, Clark Terry, Gerald Wilson); Paul Desmond Quartet (Ed Bickert).

SUNDAY AFTERNOON: The California High School All-Star Big Band (directed by Ladd McIntosh and, Don Schamber); Percy, Jimmy and Albert "Tootie" Heath; **The Afro American Suite of Evolution** by Jimmy Heath; The Olympia Brass Band.

SUNDAY NIGHT: Cal Tjader Quintet; Eje Thelin Quartet; Matrix Band; The Olympia Brass Band; Toshiko Akiyoshi – Lew Tabackin Big Band.

1977
FRIDAY NIGHT: **The Happy Birthday Monterey Suite** by Gerald Wilson (The Airmen of Note, Clark Terry, Mundell Lowe, Eddie "Lockjaw" Davis); Count Basie and His Orchestra; Joe Williams; Ted Curson Quartet (David Friesen).

SATURDAY AFTERNOON: **Mardi Gras at Monterey**: Clarence "Gatemouth" Brown; Professor Longhair and the Neville Brothers, Queen Ida and the Bon Ton Zydeco Band; The Neville Brothers; The Wild Tchoupitoulas (Big Chief Jolly).

SATURDAY NIGHT: **Twentieth Anniversary Blowout** (Harry "Sweets" Edison, Benny Golson, John Lewis, Mundell Lowe, Clark Terry, Cal Tjader, "Go" Yamamoto); Carrie Smith; Horace Silver Quintet; John Lewis and Hank Jones; The Airmen of Note.

SUNDAY AFTERNOON:California High School All-Star Big Band (directed by Benny Golson and Don Schamber); **The Contemporary Keyboard Suite** by George Duke; **Percussion Profiles** (George Gruntz, Jack DeJohnette).

SUNDAY NIGHT: The Aldeberts (Billy Childs); Art Blakey and the Jazz Messengers; Betty Carter; Matrix; Tito Puente and His Orchestra.

1978
FRIDAY NIGHT: **Same Place – New Faces**: Billy Cobham; Bob Dorough; Dexter Gordon Quartet (George Cables); Grover Mitchell and Groove; Buddy Collette; Ruth Brown with the Festival Quartet.

SATURDAY AFTERNOON: Clifton Chenier; John Hammond; Little Willie Littlefield Trio; Son Seals Blues Band (Albert Collins).

SATURDAY NIGHT: **Dizzy and Friends**: Dizzy Gillespie Quartet (Ray Brown, Arnett Cobb, Arne Domnerus, Al Haig, J.C. Heard, Milt Jackson, James Moody, Buddy Tate, Trummy Young, Sheyvonne Wright); Eiji Kitamura; Willie Bobo Latin Jazz Band.

SUNDAY AFTERNOON:California High School All-Star Big Band (directed by Don Schamber, works by David Friesen, Bengt Hallberg, Thad Jones, Mel Lewis), Kenny Burrell.

SUNDAY NIGHT: Johnny Griffin (Walter Davis); Listen Quartet (Mel Martin, Susan Muscarella); Maynard Ferguson and His Orchestra; Scott Hamilton and Buddy Tate; The Hi-Lo's.

1979
FRIDAY NIGHT: **Jazz – The International Language**: B.P. Convention Quartet from Yugoslavia (Bosko Petrovic); Davor Kajfes from Sweden; Junko Mine from Japan (Eiji Kitamura, "Sleepy" Matsumoto); Machito Y Su Orquesta from Cuba; Moe Koffman Quintet from Canada; Tete Montoliu from Spain; Victor Assis Brasil from Brazil; Dizzy Gillespie, Clark Terry.

SATURDAY AFTERNOON: **Mardi Gras Mambo – The Sounds of New Orleans**: Aaron Neville; Dr. John; Earl King; James Booker; The Neville Brothers Band; The New Orleans All-Stars; The Wild Tchoupitoulas.

SATURDAY NIGHT: **Jive with Dizzy and Friends – Part II**: Dizzy Gillespie Quartet (Slide Hampton, John Lewis, Mundell Lowe, Flora Purim, Diane Schuur, Sonny Stitt, Eiji Kitamura, Red Mitchell, Richie Cole, Bruce Forman, Scott Hamilton); Stan Getz Quintet; Woody Herman and Young Thundering Herd.

SUNDAY AFTERNOON: Berkeley High School Big Band;California High School All-Star Big Band (Woody Herman; works by Don Schamber, Dave Chesky, Clark Terry, Matt Catingub); Eagle Rock High School Combo; Young Northside Big Band (Australia).

SUNDAY NIGHT: Helen Humes; Joe Williams and Prez Conference; John Lewis and Hank Jones; The Buddy Rich Band; Woody Shaw Quintet.

1980
FRIDAY NIGHT: **Scenes –Like Old Times**: Cal Tjader Sextet; Dave Brubeck Quartet (Jerry Bergonzi); Monterey Jazz Festival All-Stars (John Lewis, Buddy Tate, Clark Terry, Bob Brookmeyer, Slide Hampton, Richie Cole, Bill Berry); Sarah Vaughan.

SATURDAY AFTERNOON: Big Joe Turner; Claude Williams; Eddie Vinson; Hollywood Fats Blues Band; James Cotton Band; Jay McShann; The Monterey Jazz Festival All-Stars.

SATURDAY NIGHT: Freddie Hubbard Quintet (Billy Childs); JoAnne Brackeen Trio; Manhattan Transfer; Slide Hampton; The Tokyo Union Orchestra.

SUNDAY AFTERNOON: Berkeley High School Big Band;California High School All-Star Big Band (works by Dr. Jack Wheaton, Slide Hampton, Freddie Hubbard, Bob Brookmeyer, Clark Terry); Foothill College Fanfairs; Monte Vista High School Combo; **Variance for String Quartet and Piano** by John Lewis (the Kronos Quartet).

SUNDAY NIGHT: **Hamp's House Party:** Lionel Hampton, Helen Humes; John Abercrombie Quartet; Louie Bellson Big Band; Richie Cole's Alto Madness (Bruce Forman).

1981
FRIDAY NIGHT: Bug Alley; Canadian Sons-Sets; Monterey Jazz Festival All-Stars (Cal Tjader, Vic Dickenson, Joe Kennedy, Richie Cole); Philippine Jazz All-Stars; Rob McConnell's Boss Brass Big Band; The Hi-Lo's.

SATURDAY AFTERNOON: Mark Naftalin's Rhythm and Blues Review (Luther Tucker); Esther Marrow; Etta James Band; James Cotton Band; John Lee Hooker and the Coast to Coast Blues Band; Willie Dixon and the Chicago Blues All-Stars.

SATURDAY NIGHT: **Viva! Carnaval in Monterey:** Batucaje; Flora Purim and Airto; Richie Cole and Alto Madness (Bobby Enriquez); Tania Maria; Tito Puente and Latin Percussion Sextet (Poncho Sanchez, Cal Tjader).

SUNDAY AFTERNOON:California High School All-Star Big Band (Bill Berry, Director; Clark Terry, Ray Pizzi, Matt Catingub, Rodney Franklin); Mills High School Combo; Woodrow Wilson High School Band.

SUNDAY NIGHT: Billy Eckstine; Mary Watkins Group; Monterey Jazz Ferstival All-Stars; Sarah Vaughan; Toshiko Akiyoshi/Lew Tabackin Band.

1982
THURSDAY NIGHT: **Gala Showcase Concert:** Batucaje, Ray Pizzi/Ron McCroby, Poncho Sanchez and His Latin Jazz Band, Gerald Wilson and the Orchestra of the 80s, Carmen McRae.

FRIDAY NIGHT: Cal Tjader Sextet; Dave Brubeck Quartet (Bill Smith); Dizzy Gillespie Quartet; Ernestine Anderson/Festival All-Stars; Mel Lewis Orchestra (Bob Brookmeyer).

SATURDAY AFTERNOON: Albert Collins and the Icebreakers; Etta James Band; Mark Naftalin Rhythm and Blues Revue (Eddie "Cleanhead" Vinson, Percy Mayfield, Lowell Fulson).

SATURDAY NIGHT: **Jazz, The International Language:** Arne Domnerus and Putte Wickman; Martial Solal and Christian Escoude; Monterey Jazz Festival All-Stars (John Lewis, Mundell Lowe, Shelly Manne, Rufus Reid); Romy Posadas Quartet; Takashi Ohi and Eiji Kitamura; Tito Puente Latin Jazz Big Band.

SUNDAY AFTERNOON: Aptos High School Big Band (directed by Bill Berry and Jack Wheaton, Bob Brookmeyer, Mundell Lowe, Clark Terry, Patrice Rushen); California High School All-Star Big Band; De Anza Vocal Jazz Ensemble; Dick Grove Jazz Composers Orchestra; Mills High School Combo.

SUNDAY NIGHT: Free Flight; Gail Wynters; Joe Williams; Red Rodney and Ira Sullivan Quintet; Woody Herman and Young Thundering Herd.

1983
FRIDAY NIGHT: Bobby Hutcherson Percussion Ensemble; Bobby McFerrin and Festival All-Stars; Buddy Rich Band; Poncho Sanchez Latin Jazz Band; Tania Maria.

FRIDAY NIGHT: GROUNDS STAGES: Benny Barth Trio (Marigold Hill); Bobby Hutcherson Percussion Ensemble; Poncho Sanchez Latin Jazz Band; Vince Lateano Trio.

SATURDAY AFTERNOON: Mark Naftalin Rhythm and Blues Revue with (Robert Cray Band, Bo Diddley, Lowell Fulson, Irma Thomas, Ester Jones).

Bassist Kyle Eastwood brought his quartet to the Festival in 1994 and 1996.

FESTIVAL PERFORMANCES AND PERFORMERS

In 1980 the popular Manhattan Transfer brought their vocal jazz harmony to the Festival.

SATURDAY AFTERNOON: GROUNDS STAGES: Dave Clay; Broadway Blues Band.

SATURDAY NIGHT: **Guitar Summit** (John Collins, Eddie Duran, Ron Eschete, Bruce Forman, Steve Grenadier, Mundell Lowe); Bill Berry and the L.A. Band; Sarah Vaughan; Wynton Marsalis Quintet (Branford Marsalis).

SATURDAY NIGHT: GROUNDS STAGES: Bruce Forman and Eddie Duran; Dave Frishberg; Heard/Ranier/Ferguson Trio; Martha Young; Vince Lateano Trio.

SUNDAY AFTERNOON: Aptos High School Big Band;California High School All-Star Big Band (directed by Bill Berry); Eagle Rock High School Combo; Full Swing; Phil Wilson and Makoto Ozone.

SUNDAY AFTERNOON: GROUNDS STAGES: Dave Clay; Vernon Alley Trio.

SUNDAY NIGHT: Joe Williams and Festival All-Stars; Jon Faddis Band (James Williams); Mel Torme; Transit West; Woody Herman and the New Herd.

SUNDAY NIGHT: GROUNDS STAGES: Denise Perrier; PeeWee Claybrook; Ron McCroby and Ray Pizzi; Transit West; Vernon Alley Trio; Vince Lateano Trio.

1984

FRIDAY NIGHT:California High School All-Star Big Band; **A Saxophone Summit** (Benny Carter, Richie Cole, "Lockjaw" Davis, James Moody, Al Cohn); Bobby McFerrin; Ernestine Anderson; Lionel Hampton and his Orchestra; Monterey Jazz Festival All-Stars.

FRIDAY NIGHT: GROUNDS STAGES: Bobby McFerrin, Ernestine Anderson, Richie Cole, Al Cohn, James Moody, Vince Lateano Trio, Bill Jackson Trio, T-Bills, Clark Terry, Bill Berry, Slide Hampton, Smith Dobson Trio.

SATURDAY AFTERNOON: Johnny Otis Rhythm and Blues Reunion (Eddie "Cleanhead" Vinson, Etta James, Big Jay McNeely).

SATURDAY: GROUNDS STAGES: Shelly Manne Trio, Full Swing (Janis Siegel), Transit West, Denny Zeitlin/Charlie Haden, J.B. and the Night Shift, Mark Naftalin's Rhythm and Blues Revue, Vince Lateano Trio.

SATURDAY NIGHT: Batucaje; Denny Zeitlin/Charlie Haden/Peter Donald; Full Swing (Janis Siegel); Richie Cole and Alto Madness; Tito Puente All-Stars with Dianne Reeves.

SUNDAY AFTERNOON: Aptos High School Combo;California High School All-Star Big Band (directed by Bill Berry, Slide Hampton, Clark Terry); Eagle Rock High School Band; Shelly Manne Trio; Transit West.

SUNDAY: GROUNDS STAGES: Eddie Duran; Mark Levine Quintet; T-Bills; Bruce Forman; Shelly Manne; Hank Jones; George Duvivier; Bobby Norris with Larry Dunlap; Bill Berry; Vince Lateano Trio; The Japanese All-Star Band (Bobby Shew); Tuck and Patty; Tubajazz Consort

SUNDAY NIGHT: Billy Eckstine, M.C.; **All-Star Festival Finale** (Eddie "Lockjaw" Davis, Bill Berry, Benny Carter, Harry "Sweets" Edison, Carl Fontana, Al Cohn, Slide Hampton, Hank Jones, Shelly Manne, James Moody, Clark Terry); Ann Patterson's Maiden Voyage; Tubajazz Consort (Rick Matteson).

1985

FRIDAY NIGHT:California High School All-Star Big Band (directed by Bill Berry); Monterey Jazz Festival All-Stars (Slide Hampton, Red Holloway, Alan Dawson, Hank Jones, Mundell Lowe, Clark Terry); The Hi-Lo's; The Modern Jazz Quartet; The Woody Herman Reunion Band.

FRIDAY NIGHT: GROUNDS STAGES: Vince Lateano Trio, Chris James Quartet, Joe Williams, The Hi-Los.

SATURDAY AFTERNOON: **Kansas City Revisited** (Linda Hopkins, Jay McShann, Buddy Tate, Big Joe Turner, Claude Williams, Al Grey).

SATURDAY: GROUNDS STAGES: Mark Naftalin's Rhythm and Blues Show; Broadway Blues Band; Mississippi Johnny Waters; Dottie Ivory; Charlie Musselwhite; Maurice McKinnies; Sonny Rhodes; Vince Lateano Trio; Linda Hopkins; P.M. Singers; Gerald Wilson Orchestra.

SATURDAY NIGHT: Dave Brubeck Quartet (Bill Smith); Gerald Wilson Orchestra; Joe Williams with Monterey Jazz Festival All-Stars; Toshiko Akiyoshi Jazz Orchestra (Lew Tabackin).

SUNDAY AFTERNOON: Aptos High School Combo; Berkeley High School Big Band;California High School All-Star Big Band (Slide Hampton, Clark Terry); Phil Mattson's PM Singers.

SUNDAY : GROUNDS STAGES: North Monterey County Elementary School Jazz Band; Vince Lateano Trio; Concert Series All-Stars; Pete Jolly Trio; Shelby Flint Group; Mundell Lowe/Andy Simkins Duo.

SUNDAY NIGHT: Poncho Sanchez Latin Jazz Ensemble; Sarah Vaughan; Woody Herman and the Thundering Herd; Concert Series All-Stars (Plas Johnson, Paul Contos, Bill Berry, Buster Cooper).

1986

FRIDAY NIGHT:California High School All-Star Big Band (directed by Bill Berry); Art Farmer – Benny Golson Jazztet (Curtis Fuller); Bob Florence and Limited Edition; George Shearing; Rare Silk.

FRIDAY NIGHT: GROUNDS STAGES: Art Farmer/Benny Golson Jazztet; Bruce Forman Quartet; Chris James Quartet; Monterey Jazz Festival All-Stars; Sue Raney.

SATURDAY AFTERNOON: Etta James; Joe Liggins and the Honeydrippers; John Lee Hooker and the Coast to Coast Blues Band; Linda Hopkins.

SATURDAY AFTERNOON: GROUNDS STAGES: Mark Naftalin Rhythm and Blues Revue (John Lee Hooker, Etta James; Joe Liggins and the Honeydrippers).

SATURDAY NIGHT: Bobby McFerrin; Bruce Forman Quartet (Bosko Petrovic, Jackie Coon, Eiji Kitamura); The Capp-Pierce Juggernaut; Monterey Jazz Festival All-Stars (Red Holloway, Jiggs Whigham).

SATURDAY NIGHT: GROUNDS STAGES: Capp-Pierce Juggernut Band; Linda Hopkins; Monterey Jazz Festival All-Stars; Richie Cole (Bruce Forman).

SUNDAY AFTERNOON: Berkeley High School Big Band and Combo; California High School All-Star Big Band; Keio Light Music Society; Monterey Jazz Festival All-Stars; Time Five.

SUNDAY AFTERNOON: GROUNDS STAGES: Bruce Forman Quartet; Jake Stock and the Abalone Stompers; **International Jam** (Eiji Kitamura, Bosko Petrovic; Keio Light Music Society Big Band); Mundell Lowe Quartet; North Monterey County High School; Richie Cole and Dianne Reeves; Time Five.

SUNDAY NIGHT: Dianne Reeves; Mundell Lowe Quartet; Richie Cole and Alto Madness (Charles McPherson, Frank Morgan); Tito Puente Latin Jazz Orchestra.

SUNDAY NIGHT: GROUNDS STAGES: Bruce Forman with Bosko Petrovic; Jake Stock and the Abalone Stompers; Jan Daneau Quartet; Keio Light Music Society; Paul Contos' Urbana.

1987

FRIDAY NIGHT: Airto Moreira and Flora Purim; Band of Rogues from Japan; Batucaje; Ray Charles; Stephane Grappelli; Toshiko Akiyoshi and Lew Tabackin Quartet.

FRIDAY NIGHT: GROUNDS STAGES: Al Plank/Vince Lateano/Bruce Forman/Larry Grenadier; Army Band – Triple Threat; Batucaje; Carol Bach-y-Rita; Paul Contos Quartet; Smith Dobson Trio.

SATURDAY AFTERNOON: B.B. King; Buddy Guy and Junior Wells; Etta James; Mark Naftalin and Blue Monday Band; Ron Thompson; Charlie Musselwhite.

SATURDAY AFTERNOON: GROUNDS STAGES: Buddy Guy and Junior Wells; Etta James; Mark Naftalin; Ron Thompson; Charlie Musselwhite, Eddie "Cleanhead" Vinson; Bobbie Reed and Surprise.

SATURDAY NIGHT: Cedar Walton Trio (Ernestine Anderson); Modern Jazz Quartet; Poncho Sanchez Latin Band; Woody Herman Band.

SATURDAY NIGHT: GROUNDS STAGES: Cedar Walton Trio; Clark Terry and Red Mitchell; Ernestine Anderson; Madeline Eastman and Monterey Jazz Festival Quartet; Poncho Sanchez Latin Band.

SUNDAY AFTERNOON: Berkeley High School Band and Combo; California High School All-Star Big Band (directed by Bill Berry, Paul Contos, Emily Haddad, Clark Terry); Mount Pleasant Singers.

SUNDAY AFTERNOON: GROUNDS STAGES: Clark Terry and Red Mitchell; Harvey Wainapel Quintet; Madeline Eastman and Monterey Jazz Festival Quartet.

SUNDAY NIGHT: Bobby McFerrin (Ron McCroby, Ray Pizzi, Toots Thielemans); Frank Morgan and Cedar Walton; Gerald Wilson Band; Monterey Jazz Festival All-Stars.

SUNDAY NIGHT: GROUNDS STAGES: Harvey Wainapel Quintet; Margie Baker and Monterey Jazz Festival Quartet; Frank Morgan and Cedar Walton.

1988
FRIDAY NIGHT: Dianne Reeves/Benny Carter/J.J. Johnson (Bill Berry and the L.A. Big Band); Timeless All-Stars; Richie Cole and Alto Madness (Emily Remler).

FRIDAY NIGHT: GROUNDS STAGES: Clark Terry with Monterey Jazz Festival Rhythm Section; Jan Deneau Quartet; Timeless All-Stars; Larry Dunlap and Bobbe Norris; Richie Cole and Alto Madness (Emily Remler); Ross Tompkins Trio.

SATURDAY AFTERNOON: Albert Collins and the Ice Breakers; Carla Thomas; Katie Webster; Maurice McKinnies; Mark Naftalin and Blue Monday Band; Queen Ida and the Bon Temps Zydeco Band; Rockin' Sidney Simien.

SATURDAY AFTERNOON: GROUNDS STAGES: Bobby Webb; Kelvin Dixon; Mark Naftalin Rhythm and Blues Revue; Queen Ida, Katie Webster, Rockin' Sidney Simien; Ron Thompson and the Resistors; Swing Twilight.

SATURDAY NIGHT: Hank Jones/Oliver Jones; Joe Williams Band; Mongo Santamaria Band; The Cheathams.

SATURDAY NIGHT: GROUNDS STAGES: Jazz Birds; John Cortes Quartet; Marcos Silva; Mongo Santamaria Band; Radcliffe Group; The Cheathams.

SUNDAY AFTERNOON: Berkeley High School Combo; Jacob Armen;California High School All-Star Big Band (directed by Bill Berry, Paul Contos, J.J. Johnson, Clark Terry); Mount Pleasant Studio Jazz Singers; Rio Americano High School Band.

SUNDAY AFTERNOON: GROUNDS STAGES: Berkeley High School Band; Clayton Valley High School Band; Eddie Duran and Madaline; Mainswing; Raj Rathor and Jim Monahan; Smith Dobson Trio (Gail Dobson).

SUNDAY NIGHT: **Big Jam** with Festival Rhythm Section (Red Holloway, Clark Terry, George Bohanon, Eiji Kitamura); Count Basie Orchestra (Dianne Schuur, Joe Williams); J.J. Johnson Quintet.

SUNDAY NIGHT: GROUNDS STAGES: Eddie Duran and Madaline; J.J. Johnson Quintet; Mainswing; Raj Rathor and Jim Monahan; Smith Dobson Trio (Gail Dobson).

1989
FRIDAY NIGHT: Batucaje; Herbie Mann and Jasil Brazz; Marcos Silva and Intersection (Toninho Horta); Tania Maria.

FRIDAY NIGHT: GROUNDS STAGES: Batucaje; Jeff Linsky; Joyce Cooling with Viva Brazil; Marcos Silva and Intersection; Monterey Jazz Festival Quartet (Madeline Eastman); Tambo.

SATURDAY AFTERNOON: Etta James and Roots Band; Jimmy McCracklin; Little Milton and His Revue; Rockin' Sidney Simien with Al Rapone.

SATURDAY AFTERNOON: GROUNDS STAGES: Ron Thompson; Charlie Musselwhite; Bobby Reed and Surprise; Little Milton and His Revue; Mark Naftalin Rhythm and Blues Revue; Maurice McKinnies; Polyhedra; Rockin' Sidney Simien with Al Rapone and the Zydeco Express.

SATURDAY NIGHT: Bill Holman Band; Freddie Hubbard Quintet (Bobby Hutcherson); Mad Romance (Louis Scherr); Monty Alexander Trio; Swing Twilight Jazz Orchestra.

SATURDAY NIGHT: GROUNDS STAGES: Eiji Kitamura Quintet; Jackie Coon Quartet; Kitty Margolis (Dick Hindman); Mad Romance; Polyhedra.

SUNDAY AFTERNOON: Amador Valley High School Big Band; Berkeley High School Combo; California High School All-Star Big Band (directed by Bill Berry; Dizzy Gillespie); Mt. Pleasant High School Vocal Group.

SUNDAY AFTERNOON: GROUNDS STAGES: David Valdez Quartet; Dos Pueblos High School Band; Jazz Jugglers; John Cortes Quartet (Scotty Wright); Kitty Margolis (Dick Hindman); Navy Showband West; Swing Twilight Band.

SUNDAY NIGHT: Eiji Kitimura Quintet; Illinois Jacquet Band; Monterey Jazz Festival Quartet (Dizzy Gillespie); Take Six.

SUNDAY NIGHT: GROUNDS STAGES: David Valdez Quartet; John Cortes Quartet (Scotty Wright); Margie Baker and Trio; Vaudeville Nouveau (Jazz Jugglers)

1990
FRIDAY NIGHT: Christopher Hollyday; Ernestine Anderson; Monterey Jazz Festival All-Stars (Tito Puente); Poncho Sanchez; Spyro-Gyra.

FRIDAY NIGHT: GROUNDS STAGES: Bob Phillips and Terry Miller; Donald Bailey Quintet; Jackie Coon Quintet; Larry Vuckovich (Claudia Gomez); Monterey Jazz Festival Quartet; Rebecca Parris; Vince Lateano and Guests.

SATURDAY AFTERNOON: **Tribute to John Lee Hooker:** Charlie Musselwhite Band; Etta James and the Roots Band; John Lee Hooker and Coast to Coast Blues Band; Katie Webster and Vasti Jackson Group;

SATURDAY AFTERNOON: GROUNDS STAGES: Al Rapone and Zydeco Express; Bluesman Willie and Yolanda Briggs; Bobbie Webb and Vivian Irving; Charlie Musselwhite Blues Band; Harvey Wainapel Quartet; John Lee Hooker; Kitty Margolis; Margie Baker; Mark Naftalin; Maurice Kemp; Maurice McKinnies; Paul Soderman and Bolder Blues Club; Ron Thompson; Yank Rachell, Katie Webster.

SATURDAY NIGHT: Gerald Wilson Orchestra; Joe Williams; Mel Brown Sextet; Oscar Peterson.

SATURDAY NIGHT: GROUNDS STAGES: Harvey Wainapel Quartet; Kitty Margolis; Monterey Jazz Festival Quartet; Norman Simmons; Virginia Mayhew and Rebecca Franks.

SUNDAY AFTERNOON: Hamilton High School Big Band; Hamilton High School Combo; California High School All-Star Big Band (directed by Bill Berry and Paul Contos); Monterey County Honor Band (directed by Don Schamber) Soquel High School Singers; Stan Getz Sextet.

SUNDAY AFTERNOON: GROUNDS STAGES: Berkeley High School Band; Bob Phillips and Terry Miller; Dos Pueblos High School Band; International Jam; Jackie Coon Quintet; Mel Martin -- Be-Bop and Beyond; Neal Finn Union Dues Band.

SUNDAY NIGHT: Dianne Reeves (Billy Childs); Dizzy Gillespie Quintet (Sam Rivers); Michel Petrucciani Group; Stanley Turrentine Quintet.

SUNDAY NIGHT: GROUNDS STAGES: Margie Baker; Mel Martin – Be-Bop and Beyond; Moonlight Jazz Band; Neal Finn Union Dues Band.

1991
FRIDAY NIGHT: Diane Schuur; Modern Jazz Quartet; Monterey Jazz Festival All-Stars (Scott Hamilton); Paquito D'Rivera and "New Band" (Dizzy Gillespie).

FRIDAY NIGHT: GROUNDS STAGES: Bob Phillips Quartet; Eddie Marshall Quintet; Helcio Milito/Weber Drummond; Jackie Coon Quartet; Larry Dunlap and Bobbe Norris; Monterey Jazz Festival House Quartet.

SATURDAY AFTERNOON: Charles Brown; Floyd Dixon with Port Barlow and Full House; Jimmy McCracklin and Linettes; Lowell Fulson Band (Mark Naftalin); Ruth Brown.

SATURDAY AFTERNOON: GROUNDS STAGES: Ann Dyer; Beverly Watson; Blues Man Willie and South Street Runners; Bobby Murray Band; Charles Brown; Darryl Rowe Trio; Floyd Dixon with Port Barlow; Jimmy McCracklin and the Linettes; Kevin Gibbs; Lowell Fulson; Mark Naftalin Rhythm and Blues Revue (Ron Thompson); Monterey Jazz Festival Quartet.

At the 1993 Festival, pianist Dorothy Donegan threatened to steal the Sunday night show.

FESTIVAL PERFORMANCES AND PERFORMERS

Vocalist Mel Torme is shown at the Festival in 1983.

SATURDAY NIGHT: Clayton Hamilton Jazz Orchestra; Eiji Kitamura Quintet with Buddy DeFranco; Jon Hendricks and Company; Shorty Rogers/Bud Shank and the Lighthouse All-Stars.

SATURDAY NIGHT: GROUNDS STAGES: Darryl Rowe Trio; Kevin Gibbs; Madeline Eastman; Mel Martin – Bebop and Beyond.

SUNDAY AFTERNOON; Berkeley High School Combo; California High School All-Star Big Band (directed by Bill Berry and Paul Contos); Chick Corea Akoustic Band; El Cerrito High School Big Band; Folsom Jazz Choir.

SUNDAY AFTERNOON: GROUNDS STAGES: Berkeley High School Band; David Valdez Quintet; Duce (Jean Fineberg, Ellen Seeling); Mel Martin Bebop and Beyond; Arne Domnerus Trio; Roosevelt High School Band; Swing Ace Band; The Dobson Family.

SUNDAY NIGHT: **Jazz from Sweden** (Harry "Sweets" Edison); Carol Sloane; Count Basie Orchestra; Phil Woods Quintet.

SUNDAY NIGHT: GROUNDS STAGES: Margie Baker Quintet; **Sax Summit** (Scott Hamilton, Red Holloway, Jack Nimitz, Herman Riley, Harvey Wainapel); Swing Ace Band; The Dobson Family; Ali Ryerson.

1992

FRIDAY NIGHT: Roy Hargrove Quintet; Tribute to Miles Davis (Ron Carter, Herbie Hancock, Wallace Roney, Wayne Shorter, Tony Williams); Yellowjackets.

FRIDAY NIGHT: GROUNDS STAGES: Ali Ryerson Quartet; Eiji Kitamura Quintet; John Cortes Quintet; Kevin Gibbs Trio; Radcliffe; Roy Hargrove Quintet; Susan Muscarella/Paul Contos Quartet; Vinx.

SATURDAY AFTERNOON: Buddy Guy; Charlie Musselwhite (Ron Thompson, Luther Tucker); Junior Wells; Katie Webster and Vasti Jackson Group.

SATURDAY AFTERNOON: GROUNDS STAGES: Bluesman Willie and So. Street Runners; Charlie Musselwhite/Luther Tucker; Junior Wells; Katie Webster and Vasti Jackson Group; Professor Blues Revue with Jimmy Dawkins; Ron Thompson and Mark Naftalin.

SATURDAY NIGHT: Betty Carter and Her Trio; Billy Childs Group; **The Music of Duke Ellington:** Lincoln Center Jazz Orchestra (David Berger, conductor; Wynton Marsalis); The Quartet (Kenny Burrell, Jimmy Smith, Grady Tate, Stanley Turrentine).

SATURDAY NIGHT: GROUNDS STAGES: Billy Childs Group; Claudia Villela/Jon Gold Group; Ed Kelly Trio; Fowler Brothers; Kitty Margolis and Dick Hindman Trio; Peter Apfelbaum and Hieroglyphics Ensemble; Steve Erquiaga Group; Weber Drummond and Zen-Blend.

SUNDAY AFTERNOON: Branford Marsalis;California High School All-Star Big Band (directed by Bill Berry and Paul Contos; Jon Faddis); El Camino High School Combo; Folsom High School Jazz Choir; Rio Americano High School Big Band.

SUNDAY AFTERNOON: GROUNDS STAGES: Ace Hill Trio; Berkeley High School Band; Big Wing Band (Japan); Folsom High School Band; New World Trio (India Cooke, Kash Killian, Eddie Marshall); Jake Stock and the Abalone Stompers; Monterey County Honor Band; Smith Dobson Jr. Quintet.

SUNDAY NIGHT: **All-Star Jam Session** (Louie Bellson, George Duke, Jon Faddis, George Bohanon, Tee Carson, Slide Hampton, John Handy); Dave Brubeck Quartet (Bill Smith); Gerry Mulligan Quartet; Modern Jazz Quartet.

SUNDAY NIGHT: GROUNDS STAGES: Big Wing Band (Japan); Buddy Connor; Eddie Marshall Band; Larry Vuckovich International-Multicultural Quintet; A Little Night Music; Nancy King and Glen Moore; Rick Hollander Quartet.

1993

FRIDAY NIGHT: Bobby Watson and Horizon; Charlie Haden's Liberation Music Orchestra (with Oakland Youth Chorus); Les McCann and Eddie Harris; Ruben Blades.

FRIDAY NIGHT: GROUNDS STAGES: Alphabet Soup; Bobby Watson and Horizon (Victor Lewis); Full Faith and Credit Big Band; Greg Abate Quartet; John Donaldson/Iain Ballamy Quartet; Monterey Peninsula Jazz Orchestra; Smith Dobson Quartet; Steve Czarnecki Quartet; Tim Volpicella Group.

SATURDAY AFTERNOON: C.J. Chenier and the Red Hot Louisiana Band; Danny Barker and Milt Hinton; Dirty Dozen Brass Band; Dr. John.

SATURDAY AFTERNOON: GROUNDS STAGES: C.J. Chenier; **Living Jazz History** (Richard Hadlock, moderator; Danny Barker and Milt Hinton); Dirty Dozen Brass Band; Johnny Nocturne Band; Michael Osborn Band; Robert Lowery and Virgil Thrasher; **The Art of Piano Trio**: Sumi Tonooka clinic.

SATURDAY NIGHT: Brecker Brothers (Mike Stern); Joe Williams; McCoy Tyner Big Band (Bobby Hutcherson); Sumi Tonooka Trio.

SATURDAY NIGHT: GROUNDS STAGES: Bobby Bradford Mo'tet; Duke Jethro Band (Nate Pruitt); Madeline Eastman; Mike Fahn Group; Ray Brown and the Great Big Band; Santa Cruz Steel; Sumi Tonooka Trio; Todd Cochran Trio.

SUNDAY AFTERNOON: Fourplay; Berkeley High School Combo; California High School All-Star Big Band (directed by Bill Berry and Paul Contos; Clark Terry); Folsom High School Jazz Choir; Rio Americano High School Big Band.

SUNDAY AFTERNOON: GROUNDS STAGES: **Jazz Trombone:** Steve Turre clinic; **My Life in Jazz:** Conversation with Orrin Keepnews (moderated by Phil Elwood); Folsom High School Jazz Band; Glenn Spearman Double Trio; Jan Deneau Trio (Lee Durley); Montery County Honor Band (Bruce Forman); Oakland Interfaith Gospel Choir; Sydney Grammer School Stage Band (Australia); Talking Drums; Zytron/James Zitro Quintet.

SUNDAY NIGHT: Charles Lloyd Quartet; Dorothy Donegan Trio; **A Tribute to Thelonious Monk, Wes Montgomery, Cannonball Adderley:** Orrin Keepnews' Riverside Reunion (Nat Adderley, Ron Carter, Barry Harris, Albert "Tootie" Heath, Jimmy Heath, Buddy Montgomery); **A Tribute to Dizzy Gillespie:** Slide Hampton and the Jazzmasters (Jimmy Heath, Paquito D'Rivera, Dianne Reeves, Clark Terry, George Mraz).

SUNDAY NIGHT: GROUNDS STAGES: Black Note Quintet; Eiji Kitamura Quintet; Mel Martin Quartet; Field Holler Jazz Orchestra (Japan); Wally's Swing World; Peck Allmond Group.

1994

FRIDAY NIGHT: **Contemporary Piano Ensemble** (Donald Brown, Geoff Keezer, Harold Mabern Jr.,Mulgrew Miller, James Williams); Marcus Miller Band; Ray Brown Trio (Benny Green, Milt Jackson, J.J. Johnson, Christian McBride).

FRIDAY NIGHT: GROUNDS STAGES: Bob Mintzer/James Williams Duo; Carmen Bradford; Charlie Hunter Trio; Dave Eshelman's Jazz Garden Band; Harvey Wainapel Trio; Josh Jones and Human Flavor; Kenny Stahl Group; Kitty Margolis; Pacific Rhy'm.

SATURDAY AFTERNOON: Angela Strehli and Lou Ann Barton; Anson Funderburgh and the Rockets; Etta James and the Roots Band; the Blind Boys of Alabama (Clarence Fountain).

SATURDAY AFTERNOON: GROUNDS STAGES: Angela Strehli and Lou Ann Barton; Anson Funderburgh and the Rockets; **Saxophone Clinic:** Bob Mintzer; Chris Cain Band; **Piano Clinic:** James Williams; Joe Louis Walker and the Bosstalkers; the Blind Boys of Alabama (Clarence Fountain).

SATURDAY NIGHT: Bob Mintzer Big Band; Joe Henderson Trio; John Santos and Machete Ensemble; Ornette Coleman and Prime Time.

SATURDAY NIGHT: GROUNDS STAGES: Black Note Quintet; Bob Johnson Quartet; David Sanchez Quartet; Eddie Gale Unit; James Williams Trio; Nnenna Freelon; Terence Blanchard Quartet (Jeanie Bryson); Wild Mango.

SUNDAY AFTERNOON: Grover Washington Jr.;Berkeley High School Combo; California High School All-Star Big Band (directed by Bill Berry and Paul Contos; Bob Mintzer and James Williams); Mount Pleasant High School Jazz Singers; Santa Barbara High School Big Band.

SUNDAY AFTERNOON: GROUNDS STAGES: Ann Dyer and No Good Time Fairies; Brass Machine (Australia); **The Life of Jimmy Lyons,** panel moderated by Ernie Beyl; **A Conversation with Max Roach**, moderated by Herb Wong; Davis High School Jazz Band; Electric Fourcast (Norbert Stachel); Global Jazz Orchestra (Japan); John Tchicai and the Archetypes; Kyle Eastwood Quartet; Monterey County Honor Band.

SUNDAY NIGHT: **"Concerto for Piano and Jazz Chamber Orchestra"** by Billy Childs; Max Roach and M'Boom; Shirley Horn Trio; Sonny Rollins.

SUNDAY NIGHT: GROUNDS STAGES: Bobbe Norris and Larry Dunlap; Eiji Kitamura; Jessica Williams Trio; Monterey Jazz Festival Clinicians; The Dolphins (Dan Brubeck); Swing Fever; Either Orchestra; Dottie Dodgion Trio.

1995

FRIDAY NIGHT: Gene Harris Quartet (Ron Eschete); John Scofield Quartet with Eddie Harris; Latin Legends (Larry Harlow, Giovanni Hidalgo, Adalberto Santiago, Yomo Toro, Dave Valentin).

FRIDAY NIGHT: GROUNDS STAGES: Cecilia Coleman Quintet; Dick Whittington Trio; **Tribute to Johnny "Hammond" Smith - Organ Jam** (Dr. Lonnie Smith, Ronnie Foster, Bill Heid); Madeline Eastman; Mary Stallings and Trio; Mel Martin – Bebop and Beyond; Ray Obiedo; Rhythm and Rhyme with Wayne Wallace; Roger Eddy Group; Wally Schnalle Group .

SATURDAY AFTERNOON: Joe Louis Walker and the Bosstalkers; Maceo Parker; Solomon Burke; Staple Singers.

SATURDAY AFTERNOON: GROUNDS STAGES: **Words and Music:** Al Young and Nathaniel Mackey; Carol Fran/Clarence Hollimon Band; Joe Louis Walker and the Bosstalkers; Maceo Parker; Martin Simpson; Ronnie Earl and the Broadcasters.

SATURDAY NIGHT: Chick Corea Quartet; Kevin Mahogany and Trio; **Scenes From Childhood** by Maria Schneider; (Maria Schneider Jazz Orchestra); Rebecca Parris; Stephane Grappelli.

SATURDAY NIGHT: GROUNDS STAGES: Dawan Muhammad and LifeForce; Joyce Cooling Group; Kevin Mahogany and Trio; Lou Donaldson Quartet; Mark Isham Quintet; Mingus Amungus; Paul Hanson and the Lost Leaders; Valerie Capers; Eddie Marshall and New Flavor; Rebecca Parris; Maria Schneider Jazz Orchestra (Toots Thielemans).

SUNDAY AFTERNOON: Lee Ritenour/Dave Grusin All-Stars; California High School All-Star Big Band (directed by Bill Berry and Paul Contos; Maria Schneider and Rebecca Parris); Rio Americano High School Big Band.

SUNDAY AFTERNOON: GROUNDS STAGES: **The Musical Genius of Duke Ellington** (panel with Dan Morgenstern, Dr. John Edward Hasse, Stanley and Helen Oakley Dance, Bill Berry, Buster Cooper, moderated by Richard Hadlock); **Beyond Category: The Life and Genius of Duke Ellington** (Dr. John Edward Hasse); Graham Connah Group; Pembroke Band (from Australia); Sonny Simmons Trio; **The Art of Vocal Jazz:** Rebecca Parris clinic; **Concepts of Jazz Arranging:** Maria Schneider clinic; King Taco; Berkeley High School Big Band; Folsom High School Jazz Choir; Bullard High School Big Band; Monterey County Honor Band.

SUNDAY NIGHT: Toots Thielemans Brasil Project; Bobby McFerrin and Bang! Zoom; Charlie Hunter Trio; Steve Turre and Sanctified Shells.

SUNDAY NIGHT: GROUNDS STAGES: Bay Area Grand Masters (Benny Barth, Tee Carson); Bill Berry/Buster Cooper Quintet; Bobby Bradford, Vinny Golia, Kimara; Charlie Hunter Trio; Denny Zeitlin/David Friesen; Jake Stock and Abalone Stompers; Nancy King and Glen Moore; Laszlo Gardony; Tom Peron/Bud Spangler Quartet; Weber Drummond/Romero Lubambo; Field Holler Orchestra (Japan); Glenn Spearman's Double Trio (Larry Ochs).

1996

FRIDAY NIGHT: **Gillespiana** by Lalo Schfrin (Carnegie Hall Jazz Band with Lalo Schifrin, Jon Faddis); Howard Johnson and Gravity!; Joshua Redman Band .

FRIDAY NIGHT: GROUNDS STAGES: Billy Mitchell Group; Claudia Gomez; Claudia Villela; Dave Douglas String Group; Ethnic Heritage Ensemble; Faye Carol (Kito Gamble Trio); Helcio Milito; Howard Johnson and Gravity!; John Cortes and Monterey; Mark Levine Quintet .

SATURDAY AFTERNOON: Irma Thomas; Johnny Nocturne Band; Otis Clay; Taj Mahal.

SATURDAY AFTERNOON: GROUNDS STAGES: Alice Arts Center Jazz Orchestra (Mike Vax); Andy Santana/Soul Drivers; Big Jay McNeeley with Johnny Nocturne Band; Henry Robinett Group; Joshua Redman Band Clinic; Robert Stewart Quartet; Roy Hargrove Clinic; Smokey Wilson; Irma Thomas; Jazz Journalists Association **Blindfold Test** with Howard Johnson.

SATURDAY NIGHT: **Evolution of the Blues** by Jon Hendricks (Hendricks, Dianne Reeves and Joe Williams); George Benson; Nana Caymmi.

SATURDAY NIGHT: GROUNDS STAGES: Dann Zinn; Eiji Kitamura; Joshua Redman Band; Kitty Margolis; Kyle Eastwood Quartet; Leon Parker Group; Leroy Jones; Peter Apfelbaum Sextet; Roy Hargrove/Billy Childs.

SUNDAY AFTERNOON: California High School All-Star Big Band (directed by Bill Berry and Paul Contos; Joshua Redman and Roy Hargrove); Yellowjackets with Lori Perry and Oakland Youth Chorus; Bullard High School Big Band.

SUNDAY AFTERNOON: GROUNDS STAGES: **A Conversation with Herbie Hancock** (Al Young, moderator), Berklee/ Monterey Quartet; Jessica Williams Trio; Jim Witzel Group; Lee Salah Band (Japan); **Jazz on Film: "Dizzy and Friends"**; Northcote College Jazz Band (New Zealand); Canberra Conservatory of Music Jazz Ensemble (Australia); Monterey County Honor Band; Santa Barbara High School Big Band; Folsom High School Jazz Choir; Project Six; Rio Americano High School Big Band.

SUNDAY NIGHT: **Autumn Sketches:** Cedar Walton and Eastern Rebellion (Oakland East Bay Symphony strings); Jon Jang Sextet (David Murray and James Newton); Herbie Hancock Quartet (Joshua Redman, Roy Hargrove and Chucho Valdes).

SUNDAY NIGHT: GROUNDS STAGES: Mel Graves Quartet; Hy-Tones (Paul Contos); Gail Dobson Group; Dmitri Matheny Group; Jon Jang Sextet; Dave Ellis Group; Ann Dyer and No Good Time Fairies; Dogslyde.

1997

FRIDAY NIGHT: Arturo Sandoval; Dave Grusin presents music from **West Side Story**; Ivan Lins.

FRIDAY NIGHT: GROUNDS STAGES: Ali Ryerson; Arturo Sandoval; B Sharp Quartet; Darrell Grant Trio; Gary Regina and Tranceport; Harvey Wainapel; Moving Pictures; Oranj Symphonette; San Franciscso Nighthawks; Tee Carson and Friends; Thomas Chapin Trio.

SATURDAY AFTERNOON: Buddy Guy; Koko Taylor and Her Blues Machine; Otis Rush.

SATURDAY AFTERNOON: GROUNDS STAGES: Duke Robillard Band; Monterey Peninsula Jazz Orchestra; Jay McShann; Rusty Zinn; Otis Rush; Rare Sounds Jazz Orchestra (Japan); Australia Youth Jazz Orchestra; **A Conversation with Gerald Wilson**; **Jazz on Film** (panel with Dave Grusin and Clint Eastwood); **Conversation with Jay McShann**; Marshall Arts Trio.

SATURDAY NIGHT: Don Byron's "Bug Music"; Jim Hall Quartet with brass ensemble featuring Claudio Roditi; Charlie Haden's Quartet West with string orchestra.

SATURDAY NIGHT: GROUNDS STAGES: John Santos and Machete; Michael Wolff Quartet; Mingus Amungus; Miya Masaoka Trio; SoVoSo; Don Byron's "Bug Music"; Jim Hall Quartet; Madeline Eastman; Jeff Hamilton Trio; Diana Krall Trio.

SUNDAY AFTERNOON: David Sanborn; California High School All-Star Big Band (directed by Bill Berry and Paul Contos; Patrice Rushen, Gerald Wilson, Benny Green, and Dave Ellis).

SUNDAY AFTERNOON: GROUNDS STAGES: Abalone Stompers; Norma Winstone with John Donaldson Trio; Wally Schnalle Quintet; Andy Milne; **An Insider's Look at Monterey** (Jazz Journalists Association panel); Monterey County Honor Band; L.A. Arts Combo, Choir, Big Band; Folsom High School Big Band.

SUNDAY NIGHT: Diana Krall Trio; **Theme for Monterey** by Gerald Wilson (Gerald Wilson Orchestra); Sonny Rollins.

SUNDAY NIGHT: GROUNDS STAGES: Bruce Forman and Friends; Dave Ellis; Marcus Roberts (solo, duo, ensemble); Myra Melford Trio; Benny Green Trio; The Meeting; Charlie Hunter.

Tenor saxophonist Dexter Gordon made a single Festival appearance in 1978.

PHOTOGRAPHY CREDITS

I would like to acknowledge all the jazz photographers who for the past forty years recreated the sounds and soul of Monterey jazz into the art of jazz photography. I am extremely grateful to those photographers listed below who made their work available for this retrospective work.

My thanks go to the family of the renowned jazz artist David Stone Martin and the *San Francisco Examiner* for graciously consenting to the use of David's marvelous drawings in this book.

It has been a pleasure to work with my friend and partner, Bill Minor, whose words will again live forever in jazz history – and whose Japanese I still can't understand.

The patience and helpfulness of the staff at the Monterey Jazz Festival, including Tim Jackson, Mary Piazza and Stella LePine, will never be forgotten. I am especially grateful to Festival Board member Jim Costello, who always said yes, even if what I proposed didn't seem possible.

Finally, to my wife and best friend, Kathy, whose love and support adds the light to the film of my life. *–Bill Wishner*

INDEX

INDEX

INDEX

INDEX TO PHOTOGRAPHERS

ABOUT THE AUTHORS AND DESIGNER

William Minor was the unanimous choice to write the history of the first forty years of the Monterey Jazz Festival. A noted journalist, Minor writes for numerous jazz magazines and journals, including *JazzTimes, Down Beat, Coda* and J*azz Forum*. His book, *Unzipped Souls: A Jazz Journey Through the Soviet Union* (1995, Temple University Press) recounts his trip to Russia to study the country's jazz culture just before the collapse of the communist state. Minor is a professional musician, a poet and short fiction writer whose work has appeared in many national publications. Also a visual artist, he resides with his wife Betty on the Monterey Peninsula. He is currently at work on a book about jazz in Japan.

Bill Wishner, photography editor, has been a jazz photographer for more than a decade. He is the curator of the exhibit *Visual Jazz ... the Art of Jazz Photography*, which has been shown in venues in southern California, Indiana and at the Monterey Jazz Festival. A member of the Jazz Photographers Association of Southern California, he was instrumental in the development of the Milt Hinton Award for Excellence in Jazz Photography, the only international award in the field. A longtime resident of southern California, Dr. Wishner now lives in Indianapolis where he is a professor at Indiana University School of Medicine.

Jeff Darnall, designer, has worked on several book projects for Angel City Press. With his partner Mark Samuels, Darnall owns and operates Samuels Darnall & Associates, a design/advertising agency on the oceanfront in Capistrano Beach, California. Having been art director of two high-profile sports magazines for five years, Darnall joined creative forces with Samuels to form an agency focusing on the active lifestyle and youth-driven markets. Born and raised in southern California, Darnall lives in Laguna Niguel with his wife Leslie, and their sons Grafton and Morgan.

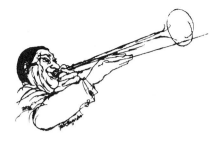

The Monterey Jazz Festival gratefully acknowledges

MCI COMMUNICATIONS CORPORATION.

Monterey Jazz Festival; Forty Legendary Years

would still be just a dream without the support of MCI.

For many years the people of MCI have been an integral part of the Festival.

Their vision and generosity have made it possible to produce this history of

America's oldest, continuous jazz festival.

The Monterey Jazz Festival and Angel City Press thank the copyright holders of the following compositions who graciously permitted the use of extended lyrics to be reproduced in this book:

Excerpts from *"The Real Ambassadors,"* Music by Dave Brubeck, Lyrics by Dave and Iola Brubeck; © Copyright 1962 and 1963 (Copyright Renewed) DERRY MUSIC COMPANY. Used by Permission of Derry Music Company.

Excerpts from *"Every Day I Have the Blues,"* Words and Music by Peter Chatman. © Copyright 1952. Renewed. ARC MUSIC CORP., FORT KNOX MUSIC, INC. and TRIO MUSIC CO., INC. Used by Permission. All Rights Reserved. International Copyright Secured.

Excerpts from *"Cherry Red,"* Words and Music by Pete Johnson and Joe Turner. © Copyright 1941, 1944, 1948 by MCA MUSIC PUBLISHING, a Division of UNIVERSAL STUDIOS, INC. Copyright Renewed. International Copyright Secured. All rights Reserved.

Excerpts from *"Saint Martin de Porres"* By Mary Lou Williams and Anthony Woods; © Copyright 1963, CECILIA MUSIC PUBLISHING CO. Used by Permission of Cecilia Music Publishing Co.

Excerpts from *"No Rollin' Blues,"* By Jimmy Witherspoon. © 1968 and 1996, POWERFORCE MUSIC (BMI). All Rights Reserved. Reprinted by Permission.